T0209320

WHEN ALL ELSE FAILS

A CHRONIC ILLNESS JOURNEY:
LYME DISEASE AND COINFECTIONS

RAVEN WRIGHT

BALBOA.PRESS

A DIVISION OF HAY HOUSE

Copyright © 2020 Raven Wright.

All rights reserved. No part of this book may be used or reproduced by any means, graphic, electronic, or mechanical, including photocopying, recording, taping or by any information storage retrieval system without the written permission of the author except in the case of brief quotations embodied in critical articles and reviews.

Balboa Press books may be ordered through booksellers or by contacting:

Balboa Press
A Division of Hay House
1663 Liberty Drive
Bloomington, IN 47403
www.balboapress.com
1 (877) 407-4847

Because of the dynamic nature of the Internet, any web addresses or links contained in this book may have changed since publication and may no longer be valid. The views expressed in this work are solely those of the author and do not necessarily reflect the views of the publisher, and the publisher hereby disclaims any responsibility for them.

The author of this book does not dispense medical advice or prescribe the use of any technique as a form of treatment for physical, emotional, or medical problems without the advice of a physician, either directly or indirectly. The intent of the author is only to offer information of a general nature to help you in your quest for emotional and spiritual well-being. In the event you use any of the information in this book for yourself, which is your constitutional right, the author and the publisher assume no responsibility for your actions.

Any people depicted in stock imagery provided by Getty Images are models, and such images are being used for illustrative purposes only.
Certain stock imagery © Getty Images.

Scripture quotations marked KJV are taken from the King James Version.
Scripture quotations marked NIV are taken from The Holy Bible, New International Version®, NIV® Copyright © 1973, 1978, 1984, 2011 by Biblica, Inc.® Used by permission. All rights reserved worldwide.
Scripture quotations marked NKJV are taken from the New King James Version®. Copyright © 1982 by Thomas Nelson. Used by permission. All rights reserved.
Scripture quotations marked NLT are taken from the Holy Bible, New Living Translation, Copyright © 1996, 2004, 2015 by Tyndale House Foundation. Used by permission of Tyndale House Publishers, Inc., Carol Stream, Illinois 60188. All rights reserved.

Print information available on the last page.

ISBN: 978-1-9822-5070-6 (sc)
ISBN: 978-1-9822-5069-0 (hc)
ISBN: 978-1-9822-5071-3 (e)

Library of Congress Control Number: 2020912981

Balboa Press rev. date: 07/17/2020

CONTENTS

When I was at the worst of this illness, I read many books. And while there were many on the physical struggle of Lyme disease and other illnesses, few spoke of the spiritual and emotional struggle. In the midst of that pain, I wished I could read something to point the way. I wanted to read about the real and honest hardship and confusion.

The realities were unpleasant, and I had a hard time finding anyone honest and open about the spiritual and emotional unhinging that this disease had left me to navigate. I was isolated and disheveled. It was a dark time.

At one point, I became about 80 percent better and then relapsed. This made me wonder how I could be throwing such an enormous amount of Western medicine at a condition and still not find lasting healing. I knew then that healing must be a total human experience. I needed more than just physical healing. I needed to heal trauma and past abuses. I had to be willing to change my entire life. And I did just that. I had to get real with and sit with a lifetime of agony and grief.

This illness was a reflection of my emotional pain. It was an opportunity to finally hear myself, to finally love myself. It really was now or never. I realized, once and for all, that although I absolutely needed medication, I could not throw pills at a broken heart.

I am hoping that this book will reveal the honest struggle and give encouragement that you too can have victories along the way to rebuilding health and happiness.

> We must not lose the urgency of this moment as
> it begs for us to begin something important.
>
> —Brendon Burchard

CHAPTER 1

Thanks to Nate!

We can hardly bear to look. The shadow may
carry the best of the life we have not lived. Go into
the basement, the attic, the refuse bin. Find gold
there. Find an animal who has not been fed or
watered. It is you!! This neglected, exiled animal,
hungry for attention, is a part of yourself.

—Marion Woodman as quoted by Stephen
Cope in *The Great Work of Your Life*

Who would've known what a gift going to an auto repair shop would be? Automobile repair—one step toward enlightenment. I was only there to replace my windshield wipers. I was pretty sure that I could do this myself, but the guys at this place had helped me with minor things many times throughout the years. The mechanic was delightful (*is* delightful). He'd been there for eleven years, and I'd seen him before. What a gift he is—to the planet.

It was a busy morning there. People were going in and out. The store was decorated with Christmas decorations. I stepped into the middle of a conversation. He wasn't just talking to me when he said, "Make a decision and don't look back."

Another man stepped forward and said, "Make *the right* decision and don't look back." But Nate's was much more inspired.

I put some tools up on the counter to purchase (they were a Christmas present; it was December 22, 2015), along with windshield wipers and mace (which doesn't work on people who are high on cocaine—this was another gold nugget of information I received from Nate). Someone said, "What if it is the wrong decision?"

He answered, "It don't matter. Just do it again. You'll get another chance, and another, until you get it right."

That would have been enough wisdom for one day, but it got better.

Another man walked in, and they spoke. They were all African American men, about fifty-five to sixty years of age. It seemed everyone in the store already knew each other. The new man said, "Every day I open my eyes is a blessing. Nothing else matters after that." This was the second time I had heard that in the last five minutes, in the same store, from two different people.

When I heard it, though, I rolled my internal emotional eyes. I had been in such pain that I had been actually wishing for death—a quick, painless one but an escape nonetheless.

I know that those words sound so ungrateful, but that day, it was true. The pain *was* too much to bear, and I was contemplating ways to end it if there was no relief.

No one knew that I was feeling this way.

I did believe that praying for a swift passing would make it happen. I was more afraid of the pain that I couldn't escape than the pain of death.

Lost in my thoughts, I think I spouted off answers in my brain, but I had never really talked to anyone out loud yet. Nate shook me out of my ruminations, almost as if he read my mind, saying as it was my turn at the cash register, "You woke up this morning. You have your life. You have money to spend. What more could you want?"

I finally spoke.

I said, "My health. I would love perfect health. I know that I look healthy, but I'm not. And I would gladly give it all away just to be well and healthy."

We walked out together at the end of the transaction, and he immediately began to talk about his family. I loved listening to him talk about his wife and kids. He was mostly talking about Christmas shopping, decorations, and food. At the end of our conversation, he said, "I don't know what you have, honey, what is wrong with your health, but—"

I don't know what made me open up. It just came pouring out.

I said, "It's Lyme disease from a tick bite about three years ago. I thought I was going to die then, and lately, I've been declining again, and I have really been wondering the same thing."

Nate was quite surprised by my admission. He said, "It's not your time. He brought you back because you have work to do, and you still have work to do." He also said not to eat chicken because it has too many hormones. He said to eat vegetables and fruit, get a Bullet blender and start juicing, and don't eat red meat. He also mentioned not eating dairy, sugars, or gluten. He gave me a lifetime of advice in fifteen minutes. I nearly cried. I gave him a hug, said "Merry Christmas," and left. That night, I ended up in the ER, and I was admitted. Without this man's words, I most certainly would have thought the absolute worst.

Two mornings later, I was able to leave the hospital. I said to God, "What's my work?" The only thought that entered my mind was *write your story*.

CHAPTER 2

This Disease Sucks!

Narcissist abuse & trauma survivors are often diagnosed
with chronic pain and autoimmune disorders because
long-term exposure to cortisol and adrenaline (fight or
flight chemicals) cause inflammation in our bodies.
Inflammation causes pain, or worse, it causes our
immune system to attack itself because it thinks the
inflammation is caused by a disease it needs to eradicate.

—Bobbi Parish, MA

Lyme disease, also called Lyme borreliosis, comes from the bite
of a tick. There are three stages to this disease. Stage 1 begins
shortly after the initial bite. Some people are not aware that they
have been bitten because the tick injects a form of anesthesia into
the person or animal its victim. I saw the tick on my thigh and had
to remove it. The first signs are a bull's-eye rash (called an erythema
migrans) at the site of the bite. Fewer than 50 percent of bite victims
ever see a rash. I did not ever have a bull's-eye rash. Soon after come
feelings of malaise and fatigue, along with chills, headache, swollen
lymph nodes, fever, and muscle and joint pain. Those who have had
this describe it as feeling as if they had the flu. I did not have any of
the flu-like symptoms. I was even watching out for them because I
knew about Lyme disease.

Stage 2 of Lyme presents over the weeks to months after the
initial bite. If it was unnoticed and untreated, the victim may begin
to feel shooting pains throughout the body, dizziness, vertigo, severe

headaches and neck stiffness due to meningitis, heart palpitations, increasing joint pain in large joints, increased muscle pain, Bell's palsy (loss of muscle tone in the face), conjunctivitis (pink eye), fainting, and skin rashes.

While I was aware of my tick bite and vigilant in my watch for warning signs, I only later learned that many do not have these early symptoms either. Thus, the spirochetes that multiply and set up residence in the host body to manifest the most harmful and persistent form of the disease were not confronted early by prophylactic medical and antibiotic care. If I had known (and I hope others will know now from my story), much of my suffering would have been avoided. However, the asymptomatic nature of my early-stage infection left me unguarded and vulnerable to the establishment of stage 3 neurological Lyme. Although mainstream medical doctors often make it difficult, victims of tick bites can obtain a three- to four-week course of doxycycline antibiotics (for children younger than nine years of age, amoxicillin is the drug of choice), which Lyme-literate physicians agree almost certainly thwart the onset of Lyme disease. I have included a list of resources in the appendix of this book to learn additional information about Lyme disease and how to treat it. If only I had known.

Current testing for Lyme is poor, and at all three stages, even the best tests can miss a positive diagnosis. Mine was always negative, and yet, I had more than forty-five of the symptoms on doctors' questionnaires. At this point, many people either do not realize they ever had a tick bite or do not attribute the many seemingly unrelated symptoms to Lyme disease. Even if you begin to suspect that Lyme disease is the cause of your myriad symptoms, as I did at the six- and eight-month marks, the tests (even the current best of the best) may show a negative result. You will be told that you do not have Lyme disease and will not receive the medical attention you need for this debilitating illness. This is what happened to me.

My Lyme disease story is slightly different because I received a clinical diagnosis when treatment finally began, and I *never* showed a positive on the Elisa, western blot, or the IGeneX titer tests. Five years into treatment, I showed a positive on one Lyme titer. Imagine, though, how many are misdiagnosed and not given care because of testing that is more than forty years old and catches only about half of the Lyme disease cases. How grateful I am that my doctors backed into a diagnosis based on an overwhelming number of clinical symptoms without a blood test. I was, however, given many blood tests to confirm a breakdown in my overall immunity. I was also given a test called a CD-57, which was only indicative of HIV, tuberculosis, and Lyme borreliosis. I had tested negative for everything else, and those tests are conclusive, while the Lyme tests are inconclusive.

At this point, weeks, months, and possibly years may have passed with no medical treatment. Stage 3, or late-stage, Lyme disease has all the prior symptoms and then adds arthritis (intermittent or chronic); severe joint pain or swelling; tingling of the hands and feet; tingling and burning sensations throughout the body and back of head; face and tongue numbness; choking on food, liquid, or saliva; worsening heart problems, including inflammation of heart tissues (pericarditis); encephalitis; memory issues; forgetting words for common items; slurred speech; mood issues; insomnia at night but severe fatigue; thyroid issues; weight fluctuations; depression; anxiety; panic attacks; and hair loss. These are just some of the manifestations.

After stages 1 and 2, Lyme disease is never *just* Lyme disease, although that would be difficult enough. There are also coinfections; the majority of Lyme disease patients report at least one, and many report having had two or more of the following coinfections (the appendix shows lists of their symptoms): babesiosis, Bartonella, ehrlichiosis, mycoplasma pneumoniae, anaplasmosis, Rocky Mountain spotted fever, tick-borne relapsing fever, Powassan viral encephalitis, tularemia, and tick paralysis. These infections can lead to DNA viruses such as the Epstein-Barr virus (EBV), varicella zoster (the shingles virus—there may or may not be an

CHAPTER 3

Fresh New Hell

> If you feel trapped, quit thinking about the
> trap and start thinking about your value.
> Life favors value. Value is your way out.
>
> —Bryant McGill

I would not have thought that at age forty-one, when I began writing this, I would not be able to work, barely be able to keep up with the laundry, and get bruises on my knuckles from playing the piano. This disease sucks, and it sucks big time.

I've come to the point where I almost cringe when someone asks me how I feel. It's not their fault—I'm sure my ego would be pissed if they didn't ask. But it's embarrassing, so I lie and say I'm fine. The embarrassment is because it never seems to be getting better. I find that others have little patience with such slow improvement.

These days, I'm *never* fine. I am always in some type of pain. Right now, as I am writing this, it's joint pain. Even my knuckles are swollen. One burns and doesn't even look normal. It's my middle finger. Maybe I can go for a drive and put it to good use, praying that it is temporary.

That's the way it is with this disease. It attacks every part of your body—sometimes at the same time, sometimes at different times.

What landed me in the hospital this time? I have been in the hospital four times and to countless doctors since the symptoms began. With side pain and nausea, feeling faint and weak, I finished icing the giant gingerbread cookie with my daughter, dropped her off at her dad's office, and drove myself to the ER.

I'm lucky. I hadn't been to the ER in years, and this was only my second time in the hospital this year. The first time, in 2015, was for a gallbladder surgery. I was told that many patients with Lyme disease end up with gallbladder dysfunction, as well as multiple organ dysfunction or failure. This, I was told, would bring a quick recovery with possibility of a quick remission at the end of the rainbow. Obviously, that did not happen. I was back in the hospital in December.

I had side pain and pelvic pain. After all kinds of tests ruled out UTI and appendicitis, the imaging showed the possible beginnings of endometriosis. This explained the pelvic pain but not the dizziness, sweating, fatigue, or weakness. I stood up to be discharged a few hours later and had to sit down and hang on to the trashcan to vomit—over and over. They felt it was not an emergency but rather a viral infection, and so they wanted to release me. I rested for fifteen more minutes for the nausea meds to take effect and tried again. This time, I got to the ER entryway. The doctor was so caring. He and the nurse walked with me. I'm positive that they don't make a habit out of walking their patients to the lobby. I was so glad that they did, though.

I did make it to the ER exit doors, and I felt so nauseated that I said, "I can't do it." My knees almost buckled. I felt the tears start to come out of my eyes.

The doctor came back, held on to me, and said, "Let's go get you a bed."

Once I was in the back, I heard him telling the other doctor on duty that I had turned green. He sat with me, and in what seemed like a panic, told the nurse to get some liquids back in me as soon as possible. She said she would do it in a minute. He grabbed the needle himself and tried to find a vein. I was losing consciousness. I felt so weak, and my situation was getting worse by the minute. No one, including me, knew what was happening. I was declining quickly.

My veins were collapsing, so he couldn't get one. I have never seen a doctor do that before. Perhaps the pelvic exam brought us closer, but he was certainly caring and so personal. He did majorly blow one of my veins, though. There was a huge bruise that lasted for well over a week. God bless him!

He had to get back to the ER, so he left. They gave me some antinausea medication that had a sedative in it. I was fading quickly. The new doctor walked in and she said, "Any other medical conditions other than chronic Lyme disease?"

Had I not already been about to pass out, I surely would have from sheer surprise. I had never heard any doctor that wasn't an LLMD (Lyme-literate medical doctor) use this term before. Most doctors in this area have not been taught much about Lyme disease. It was thought to exist mainly in the northernmost parts of the country, and many are taught that a chronic form of Lyme disease does not even exist. I didn't even mention Lyme disease to them, so it must have been in my medical records. I was amazed, and then I was asleep.

I woke up in my own room with a nurse close by.

I felt safe.

I was weak, very weak, yet I felt safe.

While it shouldn't require statement, I don't enjoy having an illness, let alone a chronic one. Perhaps, though, that is why I don't mind being in hospitals, with others who are sick, or with my own ER and ED visits, because when I'm with the doctors, under medical care, or around care, I'm safe.

I've never felt safe. Not one day, not one minute. Or maybe it was just that—minutes here and there, maybe ten minutes at a time, but not long term.

That whole "the world is a safe place" thing makes no sense to me. I wish I had believed it. I wish I believed it now. I think it is true for other people. I walked away from my church, from the music part of church services that I loved so much, from the guitar lessons that I looked forward to most weeks, and from most of the new friends that

I'd worked so hard to make. I tried so hard to be a part of that crowd. And I was included. It was great, but it came at a price. I let go of all of the things and people that I loved to create a space for myself to heal and grow on my own. This disease is so isolating. But as I have learned about this and many diseases, it changed me. Everything became clear. There was a razor-edge sharpness highlighting, once and for all, everything of real importance. I knew I had to get away from all of the things I loved, at least for a short time. I had to get away from anything that caused stress. But I also had to get away from those things that once gave me joy so that I could regroup. It became clear to me that all of it—the healthy things, people, and activities that had become my identity—was indeed poison to my life.

It was awesome, and it was awful. I got to walk away from the negative friends too, without blame. I had to leave everything and create a space for myself to heal. I was reading everything I could get my hands out about how to heal this soul-sucking and debilitating disease. Most advice was to remove myself from anything negative or stressful. I was more and more convinced that what my soul and body needed were serenity and stillness. Without these, healing would not come.

I was terrified of isolation. My brain chatter tormented me, and I simply didn't want to be alone with it. I knew, though, as my health continued to decline again, that I had to face all of it. I had to stop, turn, and face the demons I had tried to flee from my entire life. I had to let go of everything and everyone in order to heal. It was the most difficult thing that I've done as an adult. Friends that I thought would always be there did not stand the test of time. Many just did not understand that I was not the energetic, fun-loving person I once was. Others became bored and frustrated with me having an illness. Most of my friends were dealing with the same or similar illnesses and issues that I was battling daily. However, for now, I still had the support of my family. I was now truly trapped inside my body with the pain—the physical pain and the emotional pain that I carried in huge invisible suitcases everywhere I went. There was nowhere else to go. I had to face myself.

I couldn't walk away from Lyme disease, though, which I so desperately wanted to do. I couldn't walk away from my marriage, which eventually would do as well. Things were getting better. Maybe things were okay there for now. Maybe, or maybe not.

I'm weary of being afraid of my truth, or truths. Only by facing my truths would I finally begin to see that the universe loves me and that God is with me and has been by my side all along. The journey to complete and radical change had begun.

CHAPTER 4

Courage Is a Choice

We have forgotten that courage is a choice, and that permission to move forward with boldness is never given by the fearful masses. Most have forgotten that seeking change always requires a touch of insanity. If taking action before the perfect conditions arise, or before we receive permission, is unreasonable or reckless, then we must be unreasonable or reckless.

—Brendon Burchard

Once I stopped panicking, I learned to accept what is isn't so bad. Sure, I was heartbroken because of the lost friendships, relationships, and once-busy life I had led. Before Lyme (and there is a definitive before and after), I had been a working mother. I worked at a busy law firm for and with my husband. I was active with my friends. I was involved with my church in volunteer activities, food pantry, music planning, and planning for retreats, and I was a very involved mother to my little girl. I absolutely loved being a mother.

When this illness reduced my life to beds, hospitals, and pain, I was sure it was all coming to an end. I wanted to get better, but I was not sure that was going to happen.

But I was seeing that, in a very real sense, no matter what happened (or didn't happen), I would be okay. The people who were meant to be in my life would either stay in the periphery or remain intact, even if it didn't seem like it at the time. The opportunities to rejoin community, even if it was different, would be available to me again once I was well. And this time, I would know which were real and which were meant for me. I was separate from the noise, but my heart felt alone.

I didn't have to be thrilled about it. I could get angry and yell at God—and at the world—as if that would change anything. All I had to do was stop running from it. I had to hold it and acknowledge that the pain, grief, and anger was there. I don't have to like something to look at it square in the face and say, "Okay—this is what I've desperately been trying to get away from. What the hell do you want? I hate you, pain and grief, but here you are. Take a seat. Let's talk now. It sure hasn't helped to run from you. I have nowhere else to go. I'm here to listen to you. I don't like you, but I'm gonna make peace with you. What do you want to know? Let's see if there is anything here worth keeping. Had I only listened to you before, I would probably not be here now—diseased. Dis-eased."

I honestly believed I would be in remission from this illness by now. I'm into the fifth year of treatment. They said six months. When I began feeling better (after years of herxing[1] and feeling worse), I was grateful, and I drank in *every* moment of life. I hurt, but much less now, and so I ice skated, played, laughed, and roller-skated with my daughter. She was about nine years old at this time. I had been sick since she was five. I read only humorous things and watched funny shows and movies. I didn't eat meat, sugar, dairy, red potatoes, or gluten. I didn't drink alcohol. But as I started feeling better, slowly, they made their way back in. So, after the gallbladder surgery, which they assured would bring quick remission, I got worse. I thought it was because I had not kept up with the original diet and such, but there was so much more to it than that. And from there, over the course of the next couple of years, it went downhill.

---

[1] Herx, or Herxheimer reaction, is the term for an onslaught of symptoms from a die-off of the bacteria and many forms of the illness that follow a return to a regimen of antibiotics or medication to treat the disease

I thought I was truly putting this disease behind me until I nearly vomited from the pain. I'm trying not to be afraid. But I'm worried because I did beg God to let me die weeks ago when my body was in severe pain, when my heart was so broken.

Now, I'm making promises to God that I will do anything, go anywhere, leave anyone, everyone—if I can just live well with no more pain. I want to live. I want to beat this thing, these things, and I want to live *well* again!

What am I doing wrong? This is my prayer.

CHAPTER 5

Heartbreak

Hope deferred maketh the heart sick: but
when the desire cometh, it is a tree of life.

—Proverbs 13:12 (KJV)

Disappointment. That is what has caused *all* of this—the illness,
the relapse, *everything. Chronic disappointment* can make you
sick, and further, it can make you ask God for an illness and can
make you ask God for death. Sad, I know. But it's true!

Even the Bible states, "A merry heart does good like a medicine:
but a broken spirit dries the bones" (Proverbs 17:22, NKJV). I have
been broken over love—or rather, the lack of it—parental, friendship,
relationships, spousal, etc. This was not mere disappointment but
complete breakdown, and now it's physical. I can no longer say, "Oh,
it's okay. It'll get better. Oh, it's fine. I'll be fine." I can no longer
say, "They didn't mean it." I can no longer make excuses for people,
people who say they love me and don't show love, those who won't
say it or show it, people who never seem to quite give me what I
need after convincing me or conning me, sucking me and with their
charm, gentleness, humor, or whatever the hell it was.

My body and the pain that I was constantly in was telling me
again and *again* that it wasn't okay. It wasn't okay, and I was allowing
my heart to break—whether it was caused by me or someone else.
Or perhaps it was using someone else to break my heart. It will never
be okay to accept less than God's absolute best love and kindness.

It will never be okay to abuse myself. It will never be okay to allow someone else to abuse me. It will never be okay.

And it is not okay for you either!

I'm stepping back from everything that I can, noting that I wasn't even able to do some of the things I most needed to step away from at this time. I felt I had to leave home too because of the very strange vibe and lack of peace there. But I was not ready.

It was time to reevaluate.

Right now, being alone doesn't make me feel lonely. Being with people does. Again, I don't feel particularly lonely when I'm alone right now. I mainly feel lonely when I'm around others, emailing or texting others, and in groups with others. These are the main times I feel vulnerable to loneliness.

I have no idea how all this will go down. I have shut out everything and everyone important to me—except those I live with. I did not want anyone to sit by and watch me crash and burn.

Hope deferred makes the heart sick. In my case, after the chronic heartbreak came Lyme disease, mycoplasma pneumonia, endometriosis, hypothyroidism, iron and iodine deficiency, chronic global pain, POTS, fibromyalgia, crushing and unwavering fatigue (or chronic fatigue syndrome), and a whole host of other strange and disruptive symptoms. I guess the final straw of heartache was when some of my friends became strange and nonresponsive. They fell off the radar even though our friendships were solid, or so I thought. I had shared so much with them, and so I felt more vulnerable than usual. I couldn't believe that they didn't miss our friendship. Several friends became really distant. I think the strain of a chronic illness is something that many do not know how to handle. After canceled plans and my inability to be as active as I once was, our time together and the conversations became awkward.

I felt that I had to do something, and so then I shut *everyone* out, and I did so aggressively. The energy didn't lie. It was the right thing to do. The disappointment was more than I could bear. And isn't that what causes the pain every time? By admitting that lies are running your life and that the truth will turn your life on its side, you can make those first steps toward freedom!

CHAPTER 6

Love Yourself

Your life is right now! It's not later! It's not in that time of retirement. It's not when the lover gets here. It's not when you've moved into the new house. It's not when you get the better job. Your life is right now. it will always be right now. you might as well decide to start enjoying your life right now, because it's not ever going to get better than right now—until it gets better right now!

—Abraham Hicks

This is the time to love yourself.

When you're at the bottom and alone, whether because others left or because you scorched the earth and set fire to your own friends, family, and life, it's time to love yourself.

It is time to get real about it, to go after yourself the way you would a potential lover or friend. Make *you* your number one priority, because it is life or death at this point, sometimes literally. It's time to love you!

Fall in love with yourself. It's time. It's overdue, and you have reaped the backlash now of not loving yourself. How's that working for you? Now you are in the hospital or you've lost your job or you hate your life or you hate your spouse. You may be deep into addiction, or you are just overcome with depression and despair from all of it. But now, the universe is saying to you, "Will you love yourself now?"

All the distractions are just that.

All this is because you have despised yourself.

23

Are you ready to give yourself the love that I, God, want you to experience? Get quiet. Who are you? And what do you want? What would bring you happiness and fulfillment?

Don't get distracted by thoughts like "that could never happen" or "how could that happen for me?" or even "that's impossible."

"I can't get from A to B that way," you might be thinking.

Let that all be figured out by the journey. These are not your judgments to make. These will work themselves out. And here's how:

Think from the end and let God figure out the hows, the ifs, and the whens. Frankly, that part is none of your business anyway. Sit back and enjoy watching your life change. Detach from the specifics of who, what, and when. Distract yourself momentarily from the present circumstances even if that feels nearly impossible. Do it just for a moment if that is all you can do. This is the time to envision the possibilities.

But do picture, with thanksgiving, the amazing feeling of having that amazing _____. How truly great and grand would it feel to have that "thing"? This is possibly the *most* important part of creating your perfect life.

- that amazing soul, that love of your life.
- the best friend that you've missed having all of these years
- the amazing job you've dreamed of but have not pursued— yet (but you will)
- the illness healed, the perfect health you've only imagined since being hit with this illness
- the beautiful son or daughter
- the lovely new home
- the new car you feel is too selfish to wish for

Just put the picture out there into the universe, to God, as an amazing thankful prayer for the moments of pleasure, even just fantasizing about it.

And then, *let go*. That's right. Just let it go.

You can't make it from here to there, or you already would have. Hasn't there already been striving to attain your desires? If so, let the striving go.

But once you put the prayer in motion, the universe begins moving heaven and earth to get that thing, person, place, job, doctor, or money to you.

Just don't waver.

Get clear about what you want.

Freaking out and changing your mind stops the whole thing in its tracks. The universe is not emotional about your desires. It does, however, listen to your instruction. If you freak out because you aren't sure you really want that thing, person, job, etc., you are resisting the instruction you first put out there to the universe. You wonder why you're not getting it, and you become depressed because nothing ever changes. If you become afraid, slow down and continue to get clear about your true desires.

Just get clear.

1. What do you want?
2. Picture it.
3. Feel what it would feel like to have _____ (fill in blank).
4. Thank God for bringing it to you.

Think from the end.

Let go of specifics and look for signs. Then, go in the direction of your dreams and follow the signs. Signs are everywhere now. There are no coincidences. There are now only serendipitous interactions—everywhere, in every way, in every conversation, in every song, in every number, and in every advertisement.

Each moment, be thankful and grateful. God will give you what is right for you, and everything will happen in accordance with His will and in love.

If there is something you feel you shouldn't want or simply can't have, express it, picture it, appreciate it, and detach from the specifics of which person, job, or thing. Become more general in the desire itself. The truth is that you want *your* soulmate, not someone else's; you want *your* most perfect job, not a specific title at a specific place. You think you do. It has to be Joe. It has to be CEO/CFO. It has to be the dream house on the ocean.

But no, it has to be that person for you in this moment who can give and receive from you the ultimate, intimate love that you desire. Picture it as a specific him or her if you must, but open up to the possibility of someone you haven't met or that you know but haven't considered. Picture it, give thanks for it, and then detach from the specifics.

CHAPTER 7

Payoffs

> The conclusion that something is impossible is based on
> an evaluation of the resources that we possess as held in
> contrast to the size of the challenge. Yet, over and over the
> 'fact' that something is possible falls to the 'fiction' that
> it is impossible for the simple reason that our fear handily
> minimizes the former and heartedly exaggerates the latter.
>
> —Craig D. Lounsbrough

I suppose depression can become a habit, just like anything else. But being tired and sore pretty much nonstop for the last four to five months (and intermittent for five years) has gotten me down. I'm not sure that I have ever avoided people I love so much in such a startlingly obvious and destructive way.

I loved singing and playing in church, and I dropped it. I dropped guitar, which I love, with a person and family that I love. But I did it so that I could isolate and reevaluate what was healthy, to heal. I dropped so much internal drama on them, and I had to run in the opposite direction. I was in counseling at this time. I was dealing with a C-PTSD diagnosis from years of repeated and constant abuse that lasted all my young life and continued into adulthood. My amazing counselor had suggested that I start talking about the situations in my life that were causing current pain. So I began doing that, and it was so unnatural. I kept just about everything to myself, so these were unused muscles, and I felt really awkward telling others about my past and current situations. I had a hard time telling the truth about the difficulties I was really having.

I embarrassed myself by opening up to all of them, even though I should not have been embarrassed. But it's embarrassing to have a new ailment every few weeks. It's embarrassing to be a shell of the person I used to be and be falling apart at the seams. My body feels like it's collapsing, and my personal life feels like it's collapsing, and frankly, I don't want anyone else to have front-row seats to the freak show.

I was up and about for about three hours and then asleep for three. I miss *not* being exhausted and *not* hurting. What was that like? Will it ever be that way again? Surely this is temporary.

Surely this is temporary!

Yes, it's been four and a half years, but surely it is temporary.

Actually, I've been somewhat sickly my entire life. I was also surrounded by family that found it difficult to live healthy lives—physically, mentally, and emotionally. Sadly, when I try to envision myself healthy, it is difficult to picture. I wish I had a picture, a sensation, and a reality of pure, perfect health. I would love to feel good! I would give anything for it, I think.

Believe it or not, there's some reward in being ill. It's important to notice this if you have an illness. I am not at all saying that one *wants* to be sick, but there is a part of our minds that may be keeping us sick. If you have been treating an ailment for years with no real healing, unconscious beliefs may be keeping you in a holding pattern of illness. I felt that being sick gave me some feeling of safety that I could not get from myself or the people in my life as I was growing up. When I was a child, the only time that my mother would not hit me or yell at me was when I was sick. It is important to share that this is not an exaggeration. I was in a situation that was completely abusive on an ongoing, chronic basis. The yelling, screaming, and hitting happened daily, and sometimes multiple times a day. It was only when I was hurting or sick that she appeared not to be angry with me. When I was sick she gave me lots of attention that I didn't receive from her any other time. As I got older, I watched her care for my grandmother for years. She was kind to her during that time. Later, when I was in relationships with men who were unkind, I learned that when I was sick, they, too, would be easier on me.

Now, do I think that I wanted to be sick in the obvious sense of the word? Absolutely not, but since I was in relationship after relationship that was unhealthy and abusive, I had subconsciously known that illness had some safety for me. Family that would otherwise hurt me refrained if I wasn't feeling well. Let's make this *very* clear. I was *not* consciously aware of this. I did not consciously make myself ill.

However, I truly believe that the brain's biological role is to keep us alive. It is constantly trying to keep us safe and ensure that whatever it takes to keep us safe happens. Since I was actually safer when I was sick, that mentality was still running the template for my day-to-day life. Here are a few good things that can come from being chronically ill.

- You can get special attention and empathy or pity. I'll take it over no attention, but honestly, I'd rather be given attention for my musical ability, my humor, my intelligence, my looks, my boobs, whatever. I just want to be well!
- You can rest as much as you want to (at this point, I've spent so much time resting that I would love to be ice-skating or hiking—with Deet, of course).
- You can get out of things. This is huge. You can cancel anything, anytime, and receive widespread understanding. That's all great, I guess, until I have to cancel the things that I would love to be doing.

All in all, I want and wish to be well and healthy. Also, I wish I could enjoy being responsible for my own life and choices. Right now, all my decisions are solely made from a point of view of surviving. All of them.

CHAPTER 8

Don't Believe Your Abusers

We declare that we are absolved from allegiance
to those who oppress or hurt us, and that
all social connections between us and them
are and ought to be totally dissolved.

—Brendon Burchard

Writing is so difficult for me. Not the words. The words are easy! They just fall out and normally feel like they come through me, not necessarily from me. However, writing them and keeping them where it could be found by someone, putting the most important part of me down, the most intimate and private feelings—that's the difficult part. I would always write, then throw away what I had written. Before, as a child, I would get rid of it or burn it, because if I didn't, my mother would find it and read it. She did this to me when I had my own apartment as an adult as well. She always invaded my privacy. But later, when I was married, I still felt as if I couldn't keep my private thoughts on paper. I was afraid to. Even now, I have this idea that if I die, I don't want any journals that can be read. The funny thing is, I love journaling. I just can't keep a journal. I'll give the backstory on this a little later in the book.

When I was ten and my sister was nineteen, she slept in my room because my mother had remarried, and we lived in a trailer. We had a nice little house before. It was a pastel yellow, and that shade of yellow would later become my favorite color. I think I was truly happy in that home. I had peace there. I was largely left alone. My mother worked constantly, so I wasn't around her very much. My sister was my primary caregiver. She too largely left me alone because she was a teenager and was enjoying her time of peace as well. She took me swimming and to movies, then gave me a lot of space.

Before that, I lived in a semi-detached home. One side was red (or burgundy) and my side was yellow. The red side grew mushrooms in my mother's room from the floor through the dresser. Gross.

The yellow side was colonized by cockroaches and mold. We stayed sick with ear, sinus, and respiratory illnesses the entire time we were there. We didn't live there long because once the landlord realized that my mother was not going to keep paying the rent, well, they didn't want us there anymore.

In the middle of the night (or what seemed like it to me at the time—I had been asleep), my mother came bursting into the room. Seriously, *bursting*. She was angry and yelling. She did this throughout my lifetime living with her, scaring the shit out of me and my sister while we were sleeping. This time, she was coming after her. She started hitting her and yelling—screaming, actually, about some things she had written in her journal. She had written about a guy and wrote, "I wanna kiss you all over." And Julie kept yelling, "It's a song, Mama. It's just a song." She was crying and begging her to stop hurting her. It was, in fact, a song written in 1978 and performed by a group called Exile.

After that, I was always afraid she would read my stuff. And I was right: she did. You'll hear more on that most awesome moment later. I was unusually good at poetry at a young age. I always had a protective, nurturing attitude toward my writing. It was a vulnerable thing for me.

I used it to help me through some sad times. We had an assignment in the seventh grade to write a poem about the book *Where the Red Fern Grows*, by Wilson Rawls. I wrote it and many others for it and got an A on my entire poem journal. When I brought it home, she read it and said, "Are you sure that you did this by yourself? It's just too good."

I was around eleven and still in that damned trailer. What a horrible time for me. She destroyed my self-esteem in that small amount of time. I don't remember much about my early childhood. I've been told that I must have blocked it out because chunks of memories are missing from ages five to ten.

I think that I had some self-esteem prior to this, because I did believe that I could do things and do them well. But how? How, around her, could I have felt some worth, even self-love and wholeness of some kind? How, when she was a horrible, horrible troll of a woman?

And the only reason that I can come up with is that she largely ignored me and sent me away. I remember, more often than not, her motioning with her right hand, the way a cat does when it doesn't like its food, and saying, "Go to your room and play." Also, my dad was there until I was four. While he was there, he guarded me from her, and he must have given me love to some degree. The other reason I stayed somewhat intact is that she usually inflicted all of her burning self-hatred and her daughter loathing upon Julie—until Julie moved out.

She was moved into her own trailer at nineteen because my mother was insecure that her husband was attracted to her. Bleh! He would later be attracted to me (at age eleven). Eww. So many stories. They just string together like a cheap beaded necklace.

I tried my hand at drawing and spent a Christmas break morning getting Mickey Mouse in a cool background just right. I wanted to draw because my sister drew beautifully. She was told how talented she was all the time. I wanted to be told that I was good at something. I remember that it was really good, and I was pleased and surprised. I proudly presented it to my mother. She thought it was just okay, and she might have said it was good, but her face said otherwise, and I was disappointed. I believed her and put that down, waiting until much later before I tried again.

She made me sing to her. We were riding in the car together, and we had just pulled into our driveway. She said, "I can't sing well. I wish I could sing. You sing for me." I said no. She said, "Go ahead. Sing to me." I knew what she was going to do, that she was going to hurt me in some way, and I told her no again. She would actually look different when she got this way. She would look at me and, in a mocking tone, would ask me to do something. I would later learn that she was mentally ill. But I only took this in as a child. I only figured she was right and I was flawed. She got louder and said angrily, "I said to sing for me." So I did. I didn't get more than a few words out before she said, "Uggghhh, stop singing. Don't sing." I was disheartened. Could I do anything well?

So I played musical instruments instead. I started with the clarinet at eleven, then piano at thirteen, then flute, and later the guitar. But I didn't sing again in the presence of others until I was thirty-eight. I believed her. I believed her lies. Everything I ever cared about, that I was learning, I needed to keep private and not share because she would criticize and belittle it. No credit, ever.

Years later, and I'm twenty-five now. I have my own apartment, two jobs, two cats, and my independence. My mother came to visit me with my niece for a few days around Christmastime. She was about ten years old and was being raised by and abused by her grandmother too, because my sister lost her sanity with our mother and left her daughter with her. I came home from work, and my mother was particularly shitty to me (which wasn't a real shock, but it was strange, because she had only been there for a day). Later, Julie told me that she had looked for, found, and read my journal to her. What a horrible bitch!

The precious and sad part of this is that the journal was a psychological healing journey. I was seeing that I needed to begin some sort of self healing. I bought several books from a local bookstore. I was excited to heal and went right to work on the first assignment. It was to write yourself in a modern-day princess-type character. I imagined I lived in a castle and compared my family to whatever Disney or childhood story I could relate to. In this writing, I chose the *Cinderella* story. I was the princess, and I likened my mother to the evil stepmother and my half-sister and misguided friends to the evil stepsisters. The remainder of this healing journey was to write how, as an adult, I had overcome (or could overcome) this "story" and find fulfillment and success.

She read the whole thing. She read it over the phone to my (half-sister) evil stepsister. Later, my sister would tell me that it made her angry (remembering the many times her own privacy had been exploited). She said she asked her why she had been reading my things. I was an adult woman, living my own adult life with my two jobs and my cats, and I had invited her to spend some time in my cute little adult apartment to experience the life I had created without her help. Her answer? Well, she had nothing else to do.

My self-esteem had been severely affected. It was years later before I would believe that I was good at writing or singing—or much of anything, for that matter. I was in my late thirties when I heard a recording of my singing that my husband had made. It was Christmas Day. I heard it and I cried. Not that it was perfect. It wasn't. It was a little pitchy, but it was good. I'd had much musical training. Musical performance (laughably now, because I was so afraid to share it in public) was my minor in college, along with the youth ministry as a part of my religion major.

It was nice, and I did have a beautiful voice. This isn't bragging or inflating my own ego. This was a complete surprise to me. I had *always* wanted to sing. I had *always* loved music. But I had received no vocal teaching and guidance except in choir and chorus-type settings along the way.

Why else would I have learned to play so many instruments? However, I had a tremendous amount of stage fright and a true belief that I couldn't sing well. I had just learned that I could sing—and sing well. How could I not have known this? For thirty-eight years, I had not known this.

At thirty-eight, after being diagnosed with late-stage neurological Lyme disease, I began singing in front of others at my church. I was told I had a beautiful voice, not just once but over and over again. One friend said several times, "I love it when you sing."

I couldn't believe it. As I learned new truths about myself as an adult, I would often talk to her in my mind. She had been gone now for years, but I would still answer her insults. *What?* How can this be? A big red, rubber stamp down on an eleven-year-old child's life. You were wrong Dora. They were lies, all of them, and I believed you! You were wrong. What a shame! What a waste! Almost forty years that I didn't use the gifts that God had given me to the fullest because I believed my mother. She was wrong. And she was mean. How dare you, Dora!

Disgusting!

However, one enlightening question arose from this moment: What else had she lied to me about? What else could I have done? What else can I do now? I have time now. I can get to know me all over again. There may be some treasures in this beaten-up heart of mine. There would be. There have to be. There are.

There may be some hidden talents. Let's get started now at getting to know myself, this time with no criticism, this time with love and acceptance. It's not too late. *It's not too late!*

So now, even now, in my personal life, I hide the things that I write, and I throw away beautiful words because my truths have gotten me into trouble. I could only write in a few pages of the many notebooks and journals. I would have to start in the middle, never the first few pages, because those could be easily read and judged. I could easily be beaten in the middle of the night for what she had read. As an adult, I could easily be criticized and beaten emotionally, with or without my knowledge, because of the terrible betrayal of infringing on my privacy. I would throw them away out of fear. And writing, like music, was a wonderful and beautiful outlet for my pain and for expressing my joy. After reconnecting with my estranged sister, I would learn that she too still has this issue. She can only write a few pages of any journal or notebook and then must throw it away.

Still, though, when it happens—the reminders, I mean—I'm pretty shocked by them. Another truth that no one really wants to recognize—a possible repeated pattern. Once I recognized them, I could and did change them. For example, to overcome this fear and compulsion, I simply wrote my story for all to see. No more secrets. No more shame. No more fear.

I was once terrified to play music and sing in front of others. I overcame this too. I now play and sing in churches. I've led music in services. I have played for weddings, funerals, and other events. I have led music for women's retreats. This was once something that I had only wished that I could do, never realizing that it was mine already. Music, writing, the arts—that's who I am. Because of unconscious (and some consciously held) beliefs about myself, I didn't do any of these things until much later in life. But it is never too late to change an unwanted pattern!

CHAPTER 9

Don't Look Back

Transformation is not five minutes from now; it's
a present activity. In this moment you can make
a different choice, and it's these small choices
and successes that build up over time to help
cultivate a healthy self-image and self-esteem.

—Jillian Kevins

If I'm not letting emotions out, it stands to reason I am not letting emotions in either. Holding onto past emotions is a mistake. Negative past emotions create forced present and future experiences that are dark, which breeds further resentment. These repeating hopeless thoughts are the stencils for the present and future—ensuring more of the same.

In life, don't look back, whether it's hating your past or pining for what you think you remember fondly. You had trouble then too. You have just romanticized your memory. The irony is that past images are *now* a fiction—except that the repeating patterns make it real. Stop reliving your past. It isn't real. We throw our negative thoughts and fears into our future and then walk straight into it. We create our future with our past negative thought patterns and then wonder why our lives don't change and why we feel stuck, as if there is no way of creating a new, more lovely, more encouraging life. Change your thoughts, and your life will follow. Your present thoughts *are toxic.*

39

So, just think of positive past experiences. No! Why, is this dangerous? Because nostalgia is not forward moving. It is stagnant and keeps you reaching back for something that is *not* real. It, too, is a fiction, and it dangerously taints the possible joy of now. And sometimes, to take it a step further, the past likely wasn't as awesome at the time as you thought it was. Sometimes you have glorified it, and you're stealing your own joy by wishing that things are as they were then. Likely, if you could return to those moments (even the truly wonderful ones), you would remember that you couldn't be fully present in those moments either and that the problems that you have chosen to forget that you had seemed insurmountable to you at that time too.

Detachment really is the answer. Let go of all detachment to outcome. Let go of all of the clinging to a past story. Who would you be if you had not believed all the things about yourself that you either were outright taught or had come to believe in your childhood? Many of your beliefs about yourself and possibly the world around you are not true of you anymore, if they ever were in the first place. It's okay to change your thoughts. It's likely way overdue. It's quite possible that it would be a welcome change.

When I was twenty-two, I worked at an amazing summer camp. It was for youth, focusing on God. It had naturally beautiful surroundings. It was a campground tucked within a heavily wooded area. It was many miles away from the city, and the grounds were rugged and lovely. It seemed as if all the land and the setup of the camp were in order to complement the lake—and it did. The camp activities focused on great music, teamwork, and faith. A *lot* of physical activity was encouraged. This activity included kayaking, rock climbing, target shooting, and swimming. At the end of the night, deep laughing, card playing, campfires, food, and falling into bed exhausted was the normal way of life for camp workers.

I climbed to the top of a 60-foot wall to then sit on a rope and swing over the beautiful lake after a substantial freefall when a dear friend of mine said something that I'll never forget. He said, "Don't reach back after you've fallen. If you reach back, you'll rip your thumbs off." This was, in fact, true. It sounds funny now, but I was horrified. It is a perfect lesson for life, though. I'm not sure that he knew the value of this advice.

Yes, it was beautiful. Yes, it was lovely. But because you won't let it go as just one of many possibly amazing experiences, because you have made the one thing that nothing else can possibly live up to, it haunts you. But it is gone. And it is good gone, beautifully, wonderfully gone. Let it pass through your experience, because there are more amazingly beautiful, romantic experiences waiting for you. Remember, you can't even fit new clothes in a drawer or a closet if you don't remove the old ones to make room for the new. If you grab behind you, you'll miss the possibility of the joy of now, essentially ripping your thumbs off. With love.

CHAPTER 10

How Mean Are Your Thoughts?

Don't believe everything you think.

—Unknown

So, it wasn't until I was forty-one years old that it occurred to me, in a real and convincing way, that my thoughts lie to me.

My thoughts lie to me!

What?

I can't believe everything I think? Thoughts, intuition, and signs have been the only things that have led me through life. I have been making most of my important decisions from the chatter in my brain.

Wow!

I'm glad it's not too late to change that. I'm a smart person. It's not a problem to make decisions based on my thoughts. But when I tell myself I'm not liked—not loved, awkward, and unwanted—and I act according to those negative and untrue thoughts, I mess my relationships up. I just hope it's not too late. I know it's not. Mostly, I don't want to treat myself poorly. All else comes from this. Self-love is the most important love. Without it, you cannot love others. Stop deciding how people are and how people feel about you based on your thoughts. It's time to evaluate the truth of what you've believed about yourself for so long now. Are the thoughts you are thinking, which are triggering your emotions, even true?

How mean are your thoughts? I am creating my life moment by moment. What am I setting into motion? If you and I continue to

43

act according to the false narrative in our minds, we *will* miss out on the rest of our life's possibilities. The narrative that we have now or that we've had on replay wasn't true. I cannot stress this point strongly enough!

I was listening to Christmas music while playing a computer game. Karen Carpenter's beautiful voice came on, singing, "There's no place like home for the holidays." Hearing her voice, I remembered that, at one time, I had felt so inadequate in so many ways. I remembered that she had too. That's when it hit me, in a beautiful, wonderful way.

That's what your thoughts can do to you. They can kill you or make you kill yourself. Here was this amazingly talented, beautiful person. She was a drummer and a singer. She was a lovely, thin, vibrant woman with a crystal clear beautiful bell tone voice. And she began telling herself she was fat. And then she told herself that she wasn't that great of a singer and that she was worthless. What? Are you kidding me?

None of that, not *one* of those things, was true. Not one part of what she told herself had an ounce of truth to it. Did she think that she was unloved? She was so loved by almost everyone. Did she really believe she was fat? She was not fat, not for one day. But she believed the lies that her mind kept telling her until she killed herself.

She starved herself and took medications so that she could lose weight. At 110 pounds, at 100 pounds, at 80 pounds, and on down, she believed her thoughts. Now, in the after, she knows that she's loved. Now she knows she always was.

That is the power of the mind. Test your thoughts. Are they even true?

I start a new life. It began last night. It was a habit. So today has hope. I don't have to believe everything I think. My thoughts don't have to be the only driver.

I'm smart. True.

But I'm loved. I'm lovable. I'm worthy. Any thoughts that counteract these truths are lies.

New life. Day one starts now.

Intuition and signs are good go-tos when your brain lies to you. Energy doesn't lie.

CHAPTER 11

Merry Christmas, Christmas Eve!

A friend is someone who gives you
total freedom to be yourself.

—Jim Morrison

When depression sets in, it's difficult to do much of anything.

It's Christmas Eve. Because of the pain and illness, I haven't been out of the house, barely been out of my room, been somewhat out of bed, but mostly I've been watching Christmas movies and occasionally playing on the computer while listening to Christmas music.

Sounds amazing? Truly, it is. But I am completely depressed. If I still had excitement, I would be wrapping presents. I didn't even shop for my daughter this year. Granted, I was just in the hospital two weeks ago, and I have been in debilitating pain for months, but still, I wouldn't have let that slip before. My spouse did everything this year. I simply told him what I wanted to give her. I am sad.

I enjoyed the decorations and lights, but I didn't do them. I didn't send out cards this year. I didn't buy many presents at all. I have one decoration (albeit a great one) that I took out of our bathroom closet.

We had family (his family) over, and they got in their classic holiday fight over religion, politics, and economics, while I was hiding away in my room with my daughter playing computer games. I still have chest pain since last night just from having that argumentative and, in my opinion, negative energy in the house. And tomorrow there will be more "family" time.

I found myself just acknowledging and accepting the depression. I found myself appreciating *my* new ability to listen to myself and my need for separation and hiding—resting, escaping.

This is not the existence that best suits me. I found myself daydreaming and fantasizing for a hopeful, loving life filled with passion and purpose, thinking there may be real change.

Merry Christmas to you, Christmas Eve! I hope I haven't let you down this year. I did still play lots of your music on the piano and radio. I do still love your lights—beautiful lights and decorations. I do still *really* get into your movies. Thank you for all you have given me!

Historically, holidays have been some of the worst days and nights of the past thirteen years, as well as most of my life and childhood. Yes, there's still New Year's Eve and day, which have also been epic fighting days between family members, but thankfully, I managed to avoid any fights from Halloween to Christmas. This is *most* certainly a first, especially when everyone around me (including myself) is indulging.

Throughout the marriage, in its entirety, with very few exceptions, there were fights every holiday. This was true in my childhood as well. I remember a Christmas when I was a teenager. My mother, sister, and I went to a love feast at a lovely church. And when we returned home, after she had been happy, loving, and fake to everyone there, she came home and screamed at us. I don't even remember the words, just the scene and the feelings of hopelessness. Weariness fills my bones when I think of holidays and the lack of love that filled them.

I know why I would drink to deal with the emptiness. I do it to deal with all of "them" while they are doing it. I know that if they weren't around, I would only drink sparingly. I didn't start until I was twenty-eight—maybe I can be done with it as a crutch when I'm forty-eight. I don't even much like it. I use it. It is not a healthy way to deal with life. It's medicine. It's just that I don't know what else to do.

I think I've tried every escape that I could think of. None have worked. Alcohol has helped temporarily, but since it is "the" family problem, I am only feeding into it by justifying its medicinal use. I don't think there is anything wrong with drinking responsibly, but who really does that? I know some do, but I have not seen any family members who had a healthy relationship with it.

I hope to one day. I hope to be healthy with it as well.

Apparently, alcohol has always had an influence over my family, and therefore over me. I didn't know it at the time because my mother tried hard to keep that influence from us, but she was an adult child of an alcoholic, and it showed. She acted like a dry drunk and was very abusive.

I was about seven or eight years old. I didn't want to be at school. I had been sick and just wanted to be home. I went to the office, and she left work to pick me up. As soon as I got home, I got my bike out and rode around the neighborhood. She called me into the house and made me lie down. She wasn't angry. I remember wondering why she hadn't hit me for that one. My sister came home after school, and she was sick too. We shared a room and were watching a TV movie. Mom made us hot toddies. Julie was laughing because I was drunk. She was sixteen, and she was too. But I consider this a good memory. She and I were laughing, and Mom thought it was funny too.

I don't feel angry at her at the moment. I'm sure that she would've chosen differently if she had felt loved and cared for and safe. But she didn't, so she didn't. And her emotional illnesses took root. She had a mental illness, and it ruled *my* life. When she died, I think someone else stepped in where she left off. Better in ways, yes, but when alcohol rules, so does abuse.

CHAPTER 12

Chronic Illness and Faith

Give sorrow words; the grief that does not speak
knits up the o'er wrought heart and bids it break.

—William Shakespeare, *Macbeth*

I have always had a strong faith. I didn't struggle with whether or not a higher power existed. I had very little in the way of human support and care, so it was easy for me to feel comforted by the power of the unseen and nature alike. It didn't come from those it was supposed to be given by, so I somehow knew there was something bigger than me and that I could go to It for help. I knew that I could escape to nature. I knew that animals were my friends. I knew that I could pick up a Bible and the words there would bring me comfort.

I had come to see that visualizing and doubtless belief brought the change and protection that seemed unlikely in my current situation. But, somehow, my faith was slipping. I was so sick, and the One that I had prayed to for help was neither letting me be well nor letting me die to escape the prolonged pain. This was the first time, although not the only time, I would have to endure this feeling of floundering for years and years. I was angry and I felt abandoned again, only this time by the Only essence that had been my security. I remember thinking, "My faith has gone. I never thought anything would ever happen that would make me lose my belief." It, too, would be a blessing in time. It didn't feel like it, not at the time. It was time to surrender to not believing. It was time to get and be really angry for being forsaken.

Being angry and losing all hope is the thing no one ever talks about when it comes to chronic illness and death. It is a forbidden topic with many forbidden emotions. This is the reason I wrote about a dark place. There was nothing redeeming for me at the time. I was feeling completely hopeless. Nothing I had read or listened to admitted to the sheer terror of feeling like there is nothing you can do to make any of this any better.

You have to be kidding me! Epstein-Barr virus (EBV) again—or is it still? It could be chronic active Epstein-Barr virus. I didn't know anything about that until now. If the diagnosis is chronic active EBV, the prognosis is *not* good. Most mainstream doctors ignore it and write it off as no big deal. Symptoms in some subside with time, as with most viruses. In others, however, it reactivates and wreaks havoc on the immune system. It is ignored or written off largely because they do not know how or are unable to treat it.

EBV symptoms are similar to mononucleosis. Enlargement of the spleen and liver, chronic fatigue, and in rare cases, death, are just a few of them. I do know that EBV is so common that about 85 percent of the population has or has had this virus. And for Lyme patients, it is likely to be one of the many coinfections.

Part of me thought, *Well, I did get a few years prolonged from this Lyme disease treatment. I suppose I should just be thankful.*" And see, the anger goes away. What good is that?

No wonder I'm sick. I understand too much. Right after the anger passes, I just say, "Well, that sucks. How can I forgive it?" Not a good way to be, but I can't help it. I suppress my negative emotions to the point where they make me ill. I'm not allowed to get angry with God, am I? I can't cuss and cry and shake my fist, or can I? It is time to surrender my emotions. Let them go! Give them to God. Surrender to your anger, to your pain, to your truths, even when it's ugly.

He can handle my anger. I will now be honest. This is more difficult than you may think. I have been carrying a lot of resentment, anger, despair, depression, and guilt my entire adult life and probably most of my childhood as well. It is time to be raw, honest, and real. So, before I am done with the anger completely, I just want God to know something. Hold on! Here's what a real conversation with God looks like once you're ready to surrender all of the pain.

I began talking to God out loud and in my writings. I wrote things that I was taught, you could never admit to God. It was disrespectful, and frankly, I was taught that I wasn't allowed to be angry at all, much less at or about God. "God, my life has been one crapshoot, one shit sandwich after the other. You know, if I had gotten better, I was going to do so much for You! I hate You right now. I feel like I have *never* been given the chance to be the amazing me that I could have been. Everything good and successful that I've done has been in spite of any real healing, support, and headway. I am pissed at You. And I don't know if I believe in You anymore."

Is that okay to say God? Of course, who am I talking to? Who am I yelling at that I don't believe in? The fact that I'm talking to God is in, and of itself, a hint that there may be belief. But if I don't have *relief*, I have a hard time with *belief*.

I am not Job. I cannot take endless days, months, and years without any encouragement and continue to believe. Although, somehow, I have. But I feel hollow. I did believe I would get well. I did. I don't now, and at the very least, I don't know if I believe that I will recover. I hate this. Why is everything so wrong? Why? No, really, why?

I keep trying and have until that point believed that I would recover and do great things and be happy, in love, and free to be in the present moment again. That maybe at the end of this hellish nightmare of disease, I would emerge new and stronger, having learned everything I needed to enlighten me. And then there was the realization that maybe it wouldn't be okay.

Bullshit! Each day has its fresh new hell of fear and pain. What the hell? How did this happen? When will it be over? I'm too nice to stay mad for long. Why am I such a doormat, such a "walk over me now" kind of person? I'll die happy. Ha, because I don't stay angry.

Not funny, God! Only I do. I do stay angry, seething. If only I could release it, I could be healed. But it's only suppressed and repressed, and then it turns into sadness. Then the chronic sadness remains and manifests as illness. Remember, self, I deserved this. In many ways, and even directly, I felt so undeserving and miserable that I even asked for this. I feel unimportant.

Of course, I don't want to disrespect God. I have just given up pretending that I'm getting all that I need from Him. And I am especially disappointed in *His* stupid people whom I am forced to call friends. I thought that because things were so horrific for me growing up, when I was able to create my own life, it would have all been worth it. I really believed that I would have an amazing adulthood that would make all of that worth it. But I was suffering, quite possibly more than ever before. I didn't understand. I wasn't saved from it, and I could no longer even save myself.

I don't know what to do. I keep hearing that you have to have a positive attitude in order to get well, but I can't summon one up right now. A Lyme flare again, along with EBV reactivation or even worse? I'm running out of options. Everything I have tried works for a short time and then stops working.

I may have thought myself undeserving of happiness before. I may have asked to be ill as a punishment rather consciously or subconsciously, but this is what is true. I have paid my dues! I have endured enough punishment for twelve lifetimes. I should be healing and healed now. I have paid for my sins. I think I have paid for more than my sins deserved punishment for. What could I have done so horribly wrong in this life (or past ones) that I deserve to suffer so relentlessly? Even those who commit crimes get to serve time for their misdeeds and are released. This punishment—the childhood and marital abuse, the physical, emotional, sexual, and spiritual abuse endured over a lifetime—has been much worse than the crime. Not everything is positive, and not everything turns out okay.

I am out of hope and out of the will to believe God wants good things for me. There has been a long line of reasons for me to give up. Why did I ever think the *next* thing would make my life better? I think clearly now that the next thing was *not* to be better.

I've discovered that desire is part of the suffering and that getting what I thought I desired did not always make me any happier. Not only do I have a chronic illness—Lyme and company—but I also seem to have a chronic happiness issue. As in, I am never happy. And nothing helps for long.

Is there a connection between not healing the trauma of the past and not getting well from the physical disease?

CHAPTER 13

Abuse, Anger, Religion, and Illness

> I had to learn to see my shadow & hold my pain
> in its fullness with acceptance and forgiveness
> so that I could release the hate I felt for myself
> & quit hurling it blindly toward others.
>
> —Scott Stabile

I'm pretty sure that there is a connection between anger, abuse, religion, and illness. I'm not sure that there was another way for me. I think that it was the perfect storm of abuse and guilt that produced an illness. It was coming because I was sure I deserved it. It stayed because I did not heal the internal chaos, filled with fear and trauma.

I don't know how other people experience their memories, but mine seem to fade in and out, like on a movie screen. And that's how I'll recant them for you. How could I forgive all the abuse? It had to be hidden. It had to be a secret. Here's how it happened.

Physical attacks: When she would hit me, she would make sure not to leave marks or bruises on areas of my body that could be easily seen. She would grab my arms and squeeze above the arms' sleeve. She would beat my legs where pants would cover them. She would dig her nails into my head where it was covered by hair. She would pull my hair, sometimes twisting it into her fist before pulling like you would carry a trash bag out the door. She hit me in the back with her fist or would shove me down, and if there was ever a mark, she would say that it was my fault—she hadn't meant to do it.

These abusive sessions would take place until I went to college when I was seventeen, and then there would be one more attempt years later. These are just a few that stand out to me now.

The hex: She was standing at the sink in the kitchen—still in the trailer. I was about eleven. I was sitting on the couch and had my hands above my head, holding onto the back of the couch. I was just sitting there. There was no music or TV. Mom turned around and looked disgusted. I often got this disapproving look from her. I was never really sure what I had done to encite this type of seeming hate. She said, "What are you doing?"

I said, "Nothing, just sitting here."

She said nastily, "Put your hands down. Put them down. You were trying to put a hex on me."

"What? No I wasn't," I said.

Shocked, I got up and went to my room.

Weird philosophies: Riding in the car. I was sad because one of our pets had died. She said, "Dogs don't go to heaven."

"Why?" I said.

"Because they are nasty, and they drank Jesus's blood."

When I was seven, she once said, "Move away from the window. Someone can come by and shoot you in the head—to a seven-year-old. One day, as I got a little older, out of the blue, she said, "Brown-eyed men can't be trusted." Odd, but for a long time as a child, I truly stayed away from brown eyed boys and men. I thought this was simply a fact. She often told me that I was oppressed by Satan and that if I wasn't careful, I would be fully possessed by him because I had an evil side to me. I was also told frequently that I was going to hell. For a young child, this was truly terrifying. I believed that I was hellbound and that at every turn, someone would be waiting to hurt me, and she wanted me to believe I deserved it all. My worldview was shaped by someone with paranoid schizophrenia. That was, I'd learn years later, one of her diagnoses. I had no sense of reality as to what was really safe or really dangerous.

Lies about Dad: I was told that my dad had five other kids and really didn't have any use for me. I was told that he had not tried to see me or contact me. I was led to believe that he did not love me at all. I called my dad. I was twenty-six. I lived in an apartment by myself. I had broken up with my boyfriend and had two jobs and a cat, soon to have two cats. I worked at a bank, and there was a PI who banked there. I asked him to find my dad. I gave him his name, approximate age, and one of his past addresses, and I paid him fifty dollars.

I got the number and kept it for several days. I picked up the phone, shaking. I called and a woman answered. I simply asked if he was there, and she said no and that he would be home in a couple of days. She didn't ask who I was but asked if I wanted to leave my name. I told her no and hung up the phone.

A few minutes later, the phone rang. It was him. We had not spoken since I was twelve years old. I don't remember much of the actual conversation, only how sick I felt. I got off the phone and started crying, weeping, really, accompanied by this sound I can only describe as a howl filled with grief, and I nearly threw up. Good talk.

It must have been fine, because we planned a trip for me to fly out and meet them—him and his wife. He had been completely neglectful of me, which was abuse. I had grown up without a father, but I learned that she had lied to me about the times he had tried to contact me, and he let me believe that he didn't feel any love or remorse at missing out on me. I got on a plane. I didn't really know who I was meeting. I imagined I would be safe, but I didn't really know this man.

I didn't even really know what he looked like, except for in pictures that were twenty-four years old. I was so nervous on the plane that someone gave me a crystal. I do not remember it well. I just know I held onto it like my very life depended on it, keeping it as close to me as I could possibly have it.

I got off the plane and walked into the airport. Several people were standing with signs. I looked around and saw a woman whom I knew through pictures to be my stepmother. She too was holding a sign with a name on it. She was standing next to a man. That man was my father, and I recognized my dimple in his smile, but only because of the picture. The sign she was holding had a name on it, and it was my name—sort of. It was spelled wrong. My heart sank a little. How could these people not know how to spell my name? I was his daughter, for goodness' sake.

Neglect: I must have been ten years old. I got off the bus and walked up our windy gravel road that was covered in snow to discover that there was no key and that I could not get in the trailer. Neither one had left work to let me in. My mother (or stepdad) would not be home for hours, and it was freezing cold outside and snowing. My stepdad had cars, lots and lots of cars, on his 66 acres of land. I had an idea. These cars were for parts mainly. None of them could be driven, but maybe they could be started, and out of all of these, there had to be one that would start. It took some time, but reaching up underneath the seats of several cars would bring about keys. Keys would turn on engines, if they had engines. Some did. Some made no sounds. Some made sounds but did not start. Finally, one did start. I was able to turn on the engine and get some heat! Yay! And the radio worked. I was there for hours in that car, alone, before anyone came home.

I made sure I left a window unlocked in the living room for next time. And there was a next time that my mother did not leave a key under the mat. I was able to open the window—yet again in the snow—and move the couch to get into the warm trailer after school alone. I began to lock the window every day and unlock it every morning to ensure that I wasn't left again.

Then there was the time a friend of my brother jumped on me and tried to tie me down. I got free and ran up the hill into the trailer, and he beat on the door for what must have been only minutes but felt like hours to a young kid. I wonder what he might have done had he been able to get in.

The first sexual abuse: July 4, 1979, I guess. My mother and sister dropped me off at a neighbor's I had never been to. They were going to fireworks, I suppose. My neighbors had no young kids. The youngest person there other than myself was a sixteen-year-old girl. I had never met them, but my mother thought it okay to send me over there. There was a party, lots of drinking. I was being chased around by an old man pervert who was trying to tickle my vagina. I was five, and I didn't think it was okay, but the sixteen-year-old girl was laughing and running around, so I thought surely I must be mistaken. It had to be funny, right? I knew better. But the world had surely tilted on its axis. The universe must have shifted.

I finally got out of the room. I ran and got out. They tried to grab me and stop me. I left her in there, I think. A mind may be able to rewrite history that can't be handled. Either way, I know she was still in there, laughing, and I was scared to death.

My mind rewrites the story to say that I did escape, but my body knows differently. Even if I escaped that time, there were others that I did not escape from. All I know for sure is that I was four and a half years old when I was brought into that room as prey. It was light, and when I escaped from that room, it was dark. I don't remember any experience from that room, but the night and the fear didn't end there. My body remembered, and for years, I couldn't even sit with my legs apart. I always had to cross them.

Same home, same night. There is a time lapse. My memory picks back up at the other side of that door. But it was light, and suddenly, it was dark. I was scared of the dark. It was so dark outside. It was so dark inside. I had to go to the bathroom, but the house was completely dark. I turned on the light in the bathroom, and after I peed, some man began yelling. I stayed back because I got scared. The man whom I knew to be the father ran out and jumped on his teenage or twenty-something son, beating him and punching him in the back. I ran by him, hoping he wouldn't see me, with his son crying out, "I didn't turn on the light." I ran out onto the front porch. The father beat the son up because I had turned on the light.

I felt so awful for the son. Seemingly seconds later, although it must have been longer, police lights lit up the yard.

My mother and sister pulled into the driveway a few minutes later.

I can't believe my mother was so shallow and shitty to leave me with someone she did not know. Forgive her? What choice do I have? But I do have a hatred for anyone who would leave their child—and she did, everywhere, all the time. But Julie could go. She got to see fireworks that night. And I was sexually abused at age four and a half

Kitty litter: I used to have to use the kitty litter box to pee or climb out of the window to poop during the night, because I could not chance waking her up at night. She would hit me or yell. There was always so much yelling. I did this for years.

Religious abuse: I was seventeen years old. My mother told me that she had a pastor and some people from the church to pray with me and over me. I didn't think that much about it. When they arrived, though, everyone was a little strange. There were two women and two men. They asked me a few questions and gathered around me as I was sitting on the couch. There was one in a chair across from me. I think my mother was standing a little to the side, and then there were two others on the couch, one on either side. They began praying and then speaking in tongues. I sneezed, and one of them said, "There. That was a demon." I was so bewildered, I just got up and went to the bathroom to get a tissue. It took me a few days to wrap my brain around the fact that I had just been "exorcised." Seriously, my mother had told them I was possessed. Wow! It's a bit of a miracle that I believed in God at all.

Story after story. Daily dramas. Chaos. Tears, shame, and abuse reigned in my life. That was my reality, day after day after day.

Forgiveness. It is important to forgive yourself and others in your life at some point. It will have to be dealt with now or later. Other than that, I got nothin'. I got caught up here for years. This may be the reason that I could not fully heal physically. This internal work *cannot* be escaped. I tried. I thought I could get well with Western medicine alone: I relapsed. I became 70 percent better and then relapsed. The body will not heal unless and until the heart is healed.

CHAPTER 14

What Haven't I Tried?

Trust and be patient. You are making it happen,
in your own way, in its' own time.

—Scott Stabile

I have tried everything when it comes to putting this thing into remission. I have done over six years of antibiotics, supplements, vitamins. I have taken antifungals and antimalarials. I have taken IV antibiotics, IV vitamins, and minerals. I had my gallbladder removed. I had a DNC (dilation and curettage) and removal of polyps and fibroids from my uterus. My Lyme doctor told me that many with Lyme end up with these types of issues and need these treatments. I had MRIs and CT scans, an endoscopy, and a colonoscopy. I have thrown up so many times from the treatments that it would be impossible to tally it all. I have even peed in my pants, while throwing up, in front of a busy building, directly in front of a stop light, behind my own car, into a grocery bag, while my daughter was in the car because I didn't want her to see the freak show. Everyone that was there got to see it.

I had a spinal tap, which was a terrible experience. I tried spinal injections for the pain. I have taken numerous different pain medications—most didn't touch the pain. Gabapentin did. I bought a rife machine that I never used because one of my doctors said unless it was a certain type, it was a hoax. It was $2,500. A rife machine is a device that sends electromagnetic frequency into the body, usually through the hands and feet. I flew five states away to see a Lyme-literate doctor who I thought could help me, and he has. All the Lyme doctors essentially saved my life by giving me antibiotic therapies to kill the infections.

I tried ozone therapy, both rectal insufflation and IV ultraviolet ozone therapy. The nurse removes a pint or more of blood, adds hydrogen peroxide, runs it through an ultraviolet light, and then enters it back into the bloodstream. Rectal insufflation was much more effective for me personally and much less invasive.

I once went to a chiropractor who spoke a lot of chemtrails and gave me a dropper and Lyme medicine. I have done rectal ozone, and there was some relief with this. It gave me energy and an overall sense of wellbeing. There were some modalities that did improve my quality of life. Infrared sauna several times a week also felt as though it helped.

I bought an earthing mat. I do really believe in the benefits of being in touch with the healing elements of the earth. I think being grounded is important. I'm not sure if the products helped or not. I took this class which was designed to change cellular energy for healing, which was a waste of money. I have done most everything I was told to do. I tried everything I could find, no matter how hokey it may have seemed.

I did make changes that were effective as well. I completely changed my diet. After all, I feel as if food is medicine. I gave up meat, dairy, alcohol, sugar, gluten, and white potatoes for eight months and some longer. I have since added most of the above back in, but sometimes I must go back to a completely natural and clean diet. I have taken tinctures and powders and pills and thick liquids. I have put lemons in my water and sometimes limes. I drank clay, baking soda, apple cider vinegar, and even hydrogen peroxide (food grade and diluted). But there were times when I drank things that might have been considered dangerous, simply trying to get well. All these things helped me in one way or another. Many of them are still part of my lifestyle today.

I bought CBD oil and had it shipped to me. I now fully believe that it should be made available to anyone suffering with severe chronic illness and pain. I am so thankful for the ones who are willing to help others, because this has been the only relief from the pain for about a year. I was in agony and considering suicide.

I wanted you to see what great lengths I've been through to try and escape the pain. I have had many other surgeries and procedures. I had been to the ER many times in the first four years of this illness. I have seen many self-proclaimed LLMDs that did little to no good. I have driven all over the state and ended up several states away to see one of the leading doctors in the country. I have been to countless general practitioners, chasing symptoms. I have seen an orthopedic specialist, orthopedic surgeon, three ENTs, two or more OBGYNs, three integrative health doctors, two neurologists, one psychologist, two psychiatrists, two gastroenterologists, and a partridge in a pear tree.

At first, I believed a few who told me it was in my head, mere depression and anxiety. I even started seeing a counselor. He was great. I need a little counseling again, not for anxiety and depression but for the trauma of contracting and still not yet being able to shed these horrible illnesses. I knew that it wasn't just in my head, although the infection was there as well. I knew something was terribly wrong.

And I have prayed many, many prayers. And sometimes have felt His presence and knowing that I would get well and be well. And sometimes, I have felt utterly abandoned in this pit of misery and suffering. I have had so much anger and rage at this useless pain. And I have cried many tears.

Many of these attempts did not help me. More still did help and kept me alive. But at six and seven years in, I was still really struggling with pain and multiple symptoms. It hasn't been for a lack of trying and perseverance. It hasn't been that many well meaning practitioners haven't tried. So, what is the missing piece?

CHAPTER 15

Accept That You Cannot Accept

> Forgive yourself for not being at peace. The
> moment you completely accept your non-peace,
> your non-peace is transmuted into peace. Anything
> you accept fully will get you there, will take you
> into peace. This is the miracle of surrender.
> —Eckhart Tolle

I can honestly ask, is there another path for me? Is it too late? How can I give myself the love I so desperately need? I can honestly say I deserved better! I deserve better! How can I make the changes for a better life, a better existence? Do I dare? Yes, I do! How do I make these improvements in my mental and emotional situations while dealing with an all-consuming physical illness. Where do I even begin?

I don't know what my life will look like after making them. I don't really even have a crystal-clear picture of what all of those changes are. The ones I was sure that signs were pointing to have failed. Not once, not twice, but many times. How can this be? Did I not try hard enough? And therefore, this is a reason to beat myself up for failing Him, for failing myself.

Becoming a teacher was one of those things I never seemed to be able to attain because of too many obstacles. Normally, obstacles inspire me to try harder, but it became clear that these were not for that purpose. I was clearly not to be a teacher, and I accepted it. At first it felt like a failure, because everything else I had set out to do,

I was able to make those things happen. But now I know that I was saved from something that would have become a distraction.

Or perhaps the path I thought was right for me was the wrong one. It wasn't the right career choice, not the right man for me, not the right time to go, to come, to stay. To make this point, I tried to go back to school for a second degree after I graduated college with a degree in religion and music performance. I went for the winter semester, and in the summer, I was to work as a camp counselor. I went for training and became so ill that I had to leave camp. I was weak and decided to begin working. I found a roommate and moved into an apartment. I intended to take classes at night to finish the second degree.

I did very well in my first out-of-college job, a banking job, and kept getting promoted, which took up more and more of my time. I thought I would try to finish the degree in a year. One year became two, then four, then ten.

I was in my thirties and had done well in banking, so I moved on to do work in a law firm. I used my banking background later by taking care of all of the revolving accounts and financial duties. I had my daughter and found an online program that would allow me to earn an elementary education degree. I got straight A's and was close to what would be graduation. I received a call from the admissions office, letting me know that I had been put in the wrong program. Because I already had a degree, I should have been working toward the master's degree elementary education program. I was informed that none of it would transfer to that program. I was so disappointed. Two years and $10,000 later, I was no closer to becoming a teacher than I was in my twenties.

I even decided to take the Praxis and go toward the lateral entry program. I had not been to a classroom college in fifteen years. This was two to three years after the online degree debacle. I bought the books and studied for months. During this time, though, I began to feel weaker and weaker. I began to feel pain in my body. I was tired all the time. I found it really difficult even to read the pages. I went to take the test in December. I was intelligent and academically gifted. I knew this test would not be easy, but I also knew I could do it.

It had rained on my drive over. My mind didn't even feel right. I was becoming confused and discombobulated. I had a sinus infection. This would be one of many that I had in recent months. I took the test. I don't really remember much about it. My physical discomfort and mental confusion were difficult to overcome. I did not pass. I only missed it by two points.

I did not realize at the time that the physical difficulties were the beginning stages of Lyme disease. And I knew that I could have taken the Praxis again and passed it, but this was three attempts over two decades. It was clear that this was not the path for me. I realized that I wanted to be a teacher to feel a part of something, to give me a sense of belonging and feel that I had succeeded at something. I already had a degree. I already had a career, but I felt as if I had to finish this to validate myself in some way. I continued to try to obtain degrees or titles to make myself feel like I was good enough, never realizing that I was already good enough.

Even this thought leads to self-judgement: How could I have believed the wrong signs, the wrong people, or the wrong path? How could I have fallen in love with an *idea* so completely that not receiving it became my undoing?

Unraveling.

Breaking.

Broken.

The depression is large, and it's heavy. Only now, I don't have many ideas, as I have had in the past, to make it better. They, the ideas, lie to me. These groundbreaking ideas—"It'll be better when …" ideas—lie to me. So, what then? What's next? When things had not worked out in the past, I was resourceful. I could come up with another career plan or self-improvement project to prove to myself and to the world that I had value. The weird thing about this was that I was already successful in my life. This feeling was nonsense. For the first time, I was too sick to keep going, and I didn't know yet that this was an awesome beginning of understanding that everything I was already was enough. I had reached the end of myself. And what a beautiful thing that would turn out to be.

I don't think I want to accept now as my forever. What has kept me going is the thought that one day, and soon, it will all be much better. But lately, I see that believing is noble, but that belief is limiting me. It is hurting me. Weeks with this illness, turning into months and then into years, have shown me the errors of my ways. New illnesses or conditions seem to trump the misery of the ones that I had before, which I thought I could not bear.

It occurred to me that this may be as good as it gets. Now is as good as it gets. It is time to stop attaining titles and degrees to prove my worth. It is time—oddly, the time when I could physically do very little—to realize the worth that was waiting for me to finally give it a voice. I am good enough. There is nothing else to improve. It is time to be. I had to have all the distractions pulled away to stop chasing my worth. I was exhausted by the burdens of proving a value that was mine already simply because I am alive. We all have inherent value, just because we are.

CHAPTER 16

Who Am I Really?

Take each step with love and radical honesty. The path
will rise to meet your feet in most unexpected ways.

—Jacob Nordby

Some of nature's most lovely things are human emotions. There's
nothing like them, nothing more lovely, nothing more atrocious.
Love. Lust. Hatred. Anger. Resentment. Rage. Sadness. Anguish.
Joy. Gratitude. Jealousy. Loneliness. Fullness of contentment.
Satisfaction. These are all so powerful, all so unavoidable.

Yet, we act as if we can control them. We delude ourselves into
thinking that we have any power over any of these emotions. Here's
what up, kidz. In times of severe urgency, we can't even (or barely
can) control our bladders. When it's time to go, you have to go
and nothing is going to change it. If you don't go, your body will
eventually do it anyway. It will happen no matter what. What makes
us think that we can control any one of these emotions?

Why try?

Because showing any of them causes great vulnerability. And
who wants that? Because what if they don't feel the same way?
What if love isn't returned? What if I become too angry and break
something? What if I lose control?

Here's what I've learned, though. I don't become depressed
because I feel rage; I become depressed because I repress rage. I don't
feel powerless because I feel sadness; I feel powerless because I spend
energy trying to pretend that I don't feel sadness. I don't become

depressed because I have come to love someone deeply; I become depressed and sad because I refuse or am unable to show that love. I refuse to admit it. I push it down as if it has already been rejected. I become too depressed by lust, by loneliness, of any emotion because I am too afraid to admit it is there at all.

Why? These are the things that make us different. These are the things that set us apart from other living creatures. A woman at a Dr. Wayne Dyer workshop put it like this: "Frankly, we are depressed because we are too afraid to stop lying about how we really feel."

I am depressed because I have repressed most of my humanity my entire life. I am too afraid to stop lying in my life because it would be a complete upheaval. I have built a life—by all standards, a really good life. I have marriage, family, work, money, community, and friendships. But I am empty inside because this life doesn't reflect who I am at all. It just is not authentic to me.

I am depressed because I am a liar.

I am depressed because I am a fraud.

I didn't set out to be. Neither did you. In fact, I did it because I was too nice not to. I lied because I didn't want to hurt anyone's feelings, even over things like being unhappy in my jobs, in friendships, or in my marriage. I did it to my own detriment. And so did you. I so wanted the façade that I spent my entire lifetime buying into and building to be true. But my lies are not true. No matter how nice I want to be, I'll have to hurt those closest to me with my truth. I've protected others from my truth, and it has nearly cost me everything. It's life or death at this point. Maybe not literally for you but quite possibly literally for me.

This life isn't who I am.

It's a lie.

What if you look at your life and although perfect (or maybe awful, or both are possible too) and you realize it's not you. It never has been you. It never will be you. No amount of wishing can make it right for you.

So what now then?

Where do I even start? Who am I really? What do I want to say? How can I stop lying to the world? How do I *be* me? Who even am I when I don't have to please anyone else? What do I actually *like* to do instead of doing what I feel I have to do? What do I do now? I'm going to tell you where to begin, and this part really is easier than you may think.

You simply begin by telling the truth now. You can't take on the burden of going backward and trying to fix past lies—whether it's unhappiness in your job, marriage, or life. You can't fix mistakes at this point. You can only admit them. And you can only start with yourself at first. Become aware of all of your pretending.

And tell the truth. Strive to be truthful to everyone, including yourself, from this point on. That's all you do at this point. Strive to be as truthful in every situation, at every moment. This doesn't mean you have to go through and confess every unsavory thought or feeling. You don't have to go backward to try and fix the past. It simply means being as honest as possible at all given times. And if you fail, simply do better next time. Admit it to yourself, and do better next time. This is not a time for beating yourself up. It is only a time of honesty and transformation.

CHAPTER 17

Desire Is a Bitch

If something you want is slow coming to you, it can only be for one reason; you are spending more time focused upon its absence than you are about its presence.
—Abraham Hicks

Remember what it felt like to be in love. Or to want a certain job or title or home. Sometimes, this type of wanting can cause its own suffering. Not being with the Desire of your affection is miserable. What about not having and then really wanting the dream house or job? Needing and not having and wanting and not having can feel pretty rotten, actually.

For me, the Desire to be well held its own suffering, to have what I had before I contracted this disease. The regret of having taken for granted playing with my daughter without pain. I so regret not appreciating the ease of walking a mile, of walking to the kitchen some days. Before Lyme, I had a busy life, and although it was not a life that reflected me perfectly, it was full. I enjoyed my job. I often went out with my friends. My husband and I created a lively and mostly loving environment for ourselves and our family. I had hardly noticed that we were only living out his dreams. But somehow, it didn't make much difference to me at the time. I had my daughter, and I spent most of my time with her, just playing with her and enjoying her bright-eyed view of the world. Everything seems funny and downright magic to a child. My life was full of activity, and all that seemed to halt when I became ill.

Regret is its own form of self-bullying. We'll touch more on that later.

Desire is a bitch! Isn't it, though? And even though I used the word *bitch*, which denotes a feminine quality (or condition, if you're a female dog), I'm going to say that Desire is male too. Why? Because although both sexes have them, we attribute certain traits to men.

Because Desire is aggressive.

Unrelenting.

Pushy, even.

Desire causes us to pursue something until we can consume it. The nagging quality leaves it both male and female. In my own journey, I have found that unmatched Desire causes pain and most of my misery.

Most often, when we Desire something, it is out of a lack of the thing Desired. Therefore, Desire causes pain and sadness. Rarely will we have Desire for something we already have.

I hope you realize that I'm not talking about the non capitalized desire—the "want" to make your life better and improve your circumstances. I'm talking about the capital "D" Desire that kicks your ass for not having achieved this yesterday.

And I'm not saying that there can't be contentment. Contentment is a form of the opposite emotion or condition of desiring something. Contentment is gratitude for that which we already have. There is little need for change or growth when we are content.

Desire, though? It pushes you. It nags you. It screams at you that things aren't as they should be, and it begs you to make it satisfied as quickly as possible. *All else be damned.*

And it never shuts up until you give it its bottle, until you satisfy the drive that it's pushing you into. It's bigger than life. It's bigger than you. And if you can't have *that* thing, that person, that job, that child, that home, there is hell to pay. Because then Desire, the bitch that she is, will remind you incessantly that you have failed.

Most of the time, Desire reminds you why you couldn't achieve the goal in the first place. After all, it may say, "It's your fault!" It will yell at you, "What's wrong with you? You are a moron, you idiot!" And when you think it has said enough and you feel really, really low, your brain may whisper just to remind you over and over again that you probably didn't deserve it anyway.

We seek to fill the emptiness we feel when we cannot attain what we think we need or Desire. Because, see, when you can't have the Desired "thing"—be it outcome, person, job, home, or life—the temptation is to fill it with something else. We try, but it never works forever. But sure, it may for a while.

Alcohol.

Sex.

Drugs.

Other people.

Work.

Another degree.

Exercise.

Overachieving.

Making more money.

Anything to fill the hole that Desire has left unfulfilled.

I had many Desires that were unfulfilled when I fell ill. I wanted to be well. I truly Desired to feel valuable. The compulsion to seek further degrees, to play many instruments, and to volunteer for the PTA and church activities was not always a means of striving for personal growth. It was the deep and seemingly unattainable need to feel love, satisfaction, and a sense of value. I realized that I didn't even feel that within my own family life.

If Desire were a person, you would kick it out of your life. If it were a person, you would never let it have lunch with you, let alone allow it to call you a loser. And you would not live with the abuse, not a minute longer. Why, my friend, are you allowing it to come from your own mind, thoughts, words, self-destructive ways?

The Desire to be well only seems to remind of how unwell that I am. It's overwhelming and makes me feel as if it is an impossible fantasy that will never be.

But here's the thing: it may be. It may be five years, five months, five weeks, or five minutes. It may not be. But it may, and because Desire is a bitch and can only assume the worst, it is a bully, and it is, in most cases, a liar.

Mike Dooley reminds us in his book *The Top Ten Things Dead People Want to Tell You* that you've been in love before, right? You thought that you would never or could never be with that person. You got that person, didn't you? At least one of those times (Dooley 2016). The money you had to have at just the right time, the child, the home, the cure for the illness, the best friend, the hug that you needed at just the right time, the clothes, the car, the nature all around you, and God's peace flooding your heart, they came. Didn't you achieve your desires more often than not? Even the fill-ins were there for you! Although the fill-ins were not healthy avenues for dealing with your emotions, they were there.

Things have been the same for you for twenty years, but they can still change. The things you want are still likely to happen, but you may want to change the focus from Desire to desire, from attachment to detachment, from "out there" being the answer to "in here" being the answer.

Let go and let God.

Retreat.

Drop it in a heap.

Focus on you!

Be alone!

Get clear!

Ask yourself, what do I want, need, love?

Ask God, "What of these things is really best for me?"

Meditate.

"Be still and know that I am God" (Psalm 46:10, NIV).

Stop holding onto the playground equipment that flings you in a circle until you throw up, or fall, or collapse. Let it go. It will only hurt for a moment. And it may not hurt at all! It may be a salve to the soul, the healing you need, and the love you desired. It may *finally*, irrevocably, be Peace! Hear that? Peace finally. Nothing? No more chatter. No more suffering. Peace!

Detach!

Detach already!

Grieve what didn't come, and thank what didn't come. And now be open for a new way, a *real* way. A *full* way. A *healed* way. You couldn't see it before. You can now. You will now!

You will receive what your heart requires for love and peace now!

CHAPTER 18

Any Source of Betrayal Can Be Difficult to Overcome

Who gossips to you will gossip of you.

—Turkish Proverb

I have experienced so many betrayals since first getting this illness. I know that I experienced some prior to the illness. But for some reason, they seemed to increase—or maybe I was simply more susceptible to noticing the culprits. I do know now that when dealing with a chronic illness, the simple nature of the ups and downs of disease can make it difficult on those around one who is suffering the illness as well.

I began to see that illness makes people a bit strange. I think that there is a deep fear in most that they too will end up like this. If someone as healthy and seemingly successful can get something that can destroy a body so quickly, then no one is immune. And that is a scary realization for some to face. I had even been afraid that it would happen. I saw people begin to pull away from me. Many tried to invite me to things and to keep in touch, but as I began to decline in my health and ability to do things, people began to drop off. Some just stopped asking me how I was but would still come around. Some stopped asking me to do things with them because I could not be consistent either any longer. And some people just ignored me altogether. It was strange to watch, actually. If it had not been hurtful, it would have been a very interesting social study.

One person did get closer to me during this time, and when that happened, I clinged to her because everyone else was leaving. It seemed like a godsend at the time. She knew so much about the people who were part of my inner circle that I couldn't help but listen, and it was delicious. And I did share my experience, but it took a while. I didn't share it for months and months with anyone in the inner circle, but I shared it quickly with someone who would never tell anyone—or so she said.

She said, "You can trust me" and "I have your back." And, of course, she then became part of the inner circle. It was triangulation at its best. So, she and I were close for about a year.

I actually didn't question it much that she constantly spoke negatively about everyone she knew, even her husband. I didn't question it at first because I had surmised that she was just going through a difficult time and that she felt as blessed as I did to have found someone she could trust to share it with. I was so thankful for her because I was so sick and could not always do a lot of active things. She would come and sit with me while I was covered in a blanket and freezing cold because I was so thin and unhealthy at the time. She was happy—or seemed to be—to just talk with me in my home on my couch. But we would always seem to return the topic to the same two people. Gossip.

She would say, "You are exactly the kind of friend I have always wanted," but then she became strange. She began getting involved in things that I was doing. She got closer to the people that she gossiped so much about. She told me one day, "When I met you, I thought you were so beautiful and so sweet that I knew something had to be wrong with you." And so she sought me out to get to know me. She seemed to take over a part of my life for a bit and then ghosted me, completely shutting me out. It was actually really creepy. I am grateful it did not involve stalking or, well, murder. I had not experienced this kind of friendship in my adult life. I didn't know how to handle it, but now she was in my church, my life, and my friends' lives. And I felt I had to leave my own life situations for a while. I stopped music. I tried to find a new church. I tried to find new friends, but many didn't want to be friends with a sick girl who could not be counted on to follow through with events and plans. But her? She was in social media pictures with the very people she talked about so harshly. They had no idea what a deceiver they had among them.

And boy, did I suffer with the realization of all the things that I had shared. I became physically ill, truly nauseated when I saw the "I love you both" on the social media page of the person and family of the ones she had spent months spewing poison about. The "I love you so much!" comments salted the wound. It was a sad time for me. I cried many hours over this betrayal.

Gossip is a slippery slope. I thought I had overcome my need for it, the enlightened one that I was becoming. But when a seemingly sweet, beautiful, talented, smart, and fun girl came into my life while everyone else seemed to be leaving, she and I began to talk—and, oh, did we talk! The victims of her gossip were, and for years to come would remain, too foolish to realize that little Mrs. Poison was sharing details about their marriage and their conversations, then sending me pics of her now-bestie but making fun of them because they weren't the most flattering scenes. It was *Mean Girls* all over again. "They will make posts about how happy they are, but when those are the posts, you know they've always had a fight." At one point, I wanted to reach out to her. "Oh no. You don't want to make nice with her, she's crazy. She's even on medication for it. She's bipolar or something." Yet she's with them as often as she can be. So sick.

I didn't see it until it was too late. None of this was okay. First of all, mental illness is no joke. If she is bipolar or on medication, that is her business and hers alone. She also made light of her weight. At no time, in any situation, is that okay. I didn't address either of these directly. I wish I had the vision and courage to obliterate this the minute it began.

I did tell her I didn't want to gossip anymore, and bam, she was out of there. She's in their living room, and they don't even know how vicious she is. I knew instantly that it had happened to me after I saw the posts. I was now the one being made fun of. They are still friends. I see the BS posts, and I realize that I could have been a better friend to that poor girl than she ever knew. Amazing.

I grieved at the loss of the trust, at the betrayal and at the loss of the friendships. I felt extremely heartbroken, actually. I felt guilt and shame at my own behavior—at having shared and allowed such horrible things to be said to me and about those around me. I had not been a good friend to my friends, and I had not been a kind person at all. It made me want to be a better friend to people immediately. I wanted to halt all the gossip at that time. I wanted to be and to have authenticity in my relationships.

Here's the thing about gossips. If they gossip to you, then you are not safe from their harm. Be careful! Do not share your inner feelings with someone until you know they will have your back. And even then, tread lightly. Do *not* stay in the company of gossips. You cannot win with them. The best way to win is not to play. They are duplicitous at the least and completely dangerous and low energy at the worst. It is a matter of when and, not if, they will betray you. Gossip is a low vibration. It is negative in every aspect, and it will bring you down. Even if no one ever hears the things you say, the feelings and words are harmful, and they will damage your good feelings.

One more lesson that I learned from hard knocks, and which I feel is worth mentioning, is that if someone has to tell you that they are a good friend, that they are trustworthy, that they have your back, you may want to back out of the room because you may soon have a set of kitchen knives sticking in your back when you face the other direction. Someone does not have to tell you that they can be trusted. It will show in their actions, and they don't have to spend a lot of time paying lip service to an attribute they actually have. A good friend is simply a good friend. A leader is simply a leader. Someone with integrity does not have to tell you they have integrity.

A lion does not have to tell you it's a lion. It will show and it will show without question.

Before this lesson, though, I was delighted to hear information. More disturbingly, I may have felt delighted at times to hear of someone else's misfortune, out of revenge. Why? Possibly because then I wasn't alone in the drama of my own relationships. Perhaps it gave me hope in my current status. Perhaps it is simply the human condition to be curious and then to talk about it with the tribe.

If people are talking about me, that means they are interested in me. And the truth is that I am only worried about her telling certain portions of what I shared about close connections with others, because I am afraid people can see right through me. I shared way too much with this untrustworthy person. It caused me a lot of anguish and fear. It was hazardous to my mental stability at a time that my physical health was certainly flailing. Please be careful. Do not allow negative people to enter your circle. It can make your health worse as well.

> You're the average of the five people you spend the most time with.
>
> —Jim Rohn.

And I can't bear anyone, let alone *everyone*, knowing truths about me. How long have I been living a lie? Many lies? What can I do to begin being authentic? Maybe start with not gossiping. Then, I suppose, I should do the following:

1. Allow the truths, my truths, to begin coming out. Stop covering truth with lies. Even if it's uncomfortable, begin to be truthful to myself about my heart's desires. This is not something that everyone gets to know. Not everyone deserves to know what you're up to. Only those that your heart is truly safe with are deserving of your deepest thoughts. Even then, some are just for you.

2. Begin allowing love into my space. Seek and allow healing to enter in. Treat myself really well. Give myself a lot of self-love and self-care.

3. Shut down and shut out anything that does not serve me. If it is not loving and respectful, it no longer deserves a place in my life.

4. If the truth confronts me lovingly—admit and accept it. No longer fight my truths. This is God helping me to move out of the ego and away from the house of cards that I've built and into my authentic self.

5. Stop stuffing a square peg into a round hole. It's not for me. it's for you. That's why you're reading these words. The facade is admirable, but it isn't authentic. It isn't you. And it isn't me either.

All things are working together for my good. "And we know that in all things God works for the good of those who love Him, who have been called according to His purpose" (Romans 8:28, NIV). The truth needs to be lived. This is my purpose, your purpose, everyone's purpose. Specifically, our purpose is to give and receive love.

It is *not* God's will for me to live out my life well within ego or religious guidelines. Get ready to upset the apple cart. We can blow this whole life out of the water in order to create a new one, an authentic one. Go gently—in love!

CHAPTER 19

I Saved Myself for This?

I shouldn't have known better because I couldn't
have known better because I hadn't yet learnt what
I know now. Today I forgive my younger self.

—Sandy Newbigging

I surmise the reason I had trouble in relationships is that the guy I gave my virginity to (at age twenty-four) had a girl call him while I was there. I actually answered the phone. She asked to speak with him, so I handed the phone to him. He was uncomfortable, so I was more curious than I may have originally been. He was walking up the stairs. I wasn't far behind when he said, "Can I call you back?" Eventually, after much pressing, he confessed. She had gotten his number from a dating service. What?

Until now, as I was looking over this beautiful lake and park at age forty-one, I had forgotten how much that crushed me. How was I going to find out? When was he going to tell me? I was on the pill. We were monogamous, or so I thought, so we didn't use protection. I had saved myself for this? Are you kidding me?

Was he going to tell me after dating someone at the same time and sleeping with her too? Would he use protection then? Not unless I made him. I don't even know that he hadn't already been with someone. Did I mention that we were living together?

I moved out. I think I did so immediately, but that was many years ago. After that, it didn't matter much to me if I was faithful—to him, anyway. In fact, before I knew it, we were going to get engaged. A guy who I worked with sort of grabbed me, and we made out in the bank of the other job that I worked in next door. He was a bartender, and I was a hostess, and of course, he had a girlfriend. I'm pretty sure that he lived with her too.

We had gone next door to grab some extra chairs or something, and next thing I knew, his tongue was in my mouth and his hand was up my skirt, and although I had a boyfriend and almost a fiancé, I did not feel badly about it. It was the first time I had been unfaithful in any type of relationship, but I didn't feel bad after what he had done. It felt like it was just what I needed to move on, and I felt vindicated after his cheating. That was the thing right? What's good for the goose …

It should have been a huge flag to me. This was not the person I wanted to be. I needed to be out of that relationship. I felt as though they were the same men with a different face. What did I need to change to attract better men?

I knew then that there had been a quantum shift in my view of relationships, because up to that point, I had been insanely faithful to whomever I was in a relationship with at the time. But I stayed with him anyway. I felt little remorse after the shit that he had pulled, so why did I marry him?

Religious guilt. *Religious guilt!* I was sad and guilty for having had sex before marriage, so I thought if I married him, I could fix it. I loved him somewhat, as a human. But now I know that it certainly wasn't the kind of love, trust, and respect that a marriage could be built on.

I was twenty-six, not really young but very, very naive. The marriage lasted two years (plus one for the year of legal separation). That marriage was doomed from the start, and everyone but me knew it. About eight months into our marriage, things began going downhill. Maybe they had begun going downhill out of the gate. I wanted him to come and meet me at the hospital to see my mother, who was dying of cancer. He insisted that I drive all the way back and get him (very much out of the way for me, as I was working, and he had been off of work for several hours. He easily could have driven to meet me).

He said it was too far and that he could not meet me and that if I wanted him to go, I should come get him. "After all," he said, "it isn't *my* mother."

Yes, he really said that. Those were his words. I think that was the moment I left the marriage, but I continued to try. I said, "If you aren't there for me during this, I won't want to be with you when it's over."

He said, "Is that a threat?"

I wasn't fighting, yelling, or screaming. I simply said, "No. It's a warning. It's the truth. I just know myself." This was one of the more difficult things that a person could go through. This was a clear picture of this marriage. That was the moment that I unplugged from it. It took eight more months to leave.

I gave him one last chance. By this time, my mother had already died. I told him that someone was interested in me and that I had feelings for him too. I had developed feelings for someone else because he became an amazing friend to me during this difficult time. I was grieving and in need of someone to talk with so badly that I didn't even foresee that this situation was dangerous. I told him that I was willing to leave my job if he could get me on his insurance until I found another job. And he said it was too hard. Yes, that really happened too.

I was alone and vulnerable. My mother had just died, and it was only a short while before I realized my marriage was essentially over, although I couldn't leave at the time. But I was always vulnerable. I hated that part of myself. I still resent it when I'm in a vulnerable position. This has been my downfall every time. This is how I've begun too many relationships. In moments of weakness, it is best to heal before moving on. But I never seemed to do it that way.

So, I didn't have to be alone though. Robert and I first kissed in February. He kissed me. He was my boss, and we were both married. We didn't have sex for a couple of months, though. And then we left three months after that. We didn't live together right away, but essentially, that's what happened. He stayed in an Extended Stay America and I rented a room in a neighbor's condo. I don't know why I didn't see that I was just compounding a problem.

When Robert started befriending me, I didn't see where it was going at first, and by the time I did, I didn't care. He had already kissed me. I saw fun, love, and excitement, and I was ready to jump ship. And I did, only I jumped out of the frying pan and into the fire. If religious guilt had been the reason I got married before, now that I really have had a full-blown affair, how could I fix this blight? I just kept going, though, as if I were on autopilot, and I never stopped to think that this wasn't the way to heal my sense of unworthiness. It seemed he had stepped in to save me from myself and my clumsy way of filling my void. It had to be meant to be this time.

I married Robert too. Second marriage. I was thirty years old. Yes, I did at least really love him, and it did seem meant to be. I thought we would make it for the rest of our time here. We have an amazing daughter and a friendship that lasted even throughout a divorce. I do not regret this one. I just wish that I could have healed before moving on. I don't know if it would have made any difference in the ultimate outcome of a second divorce. But I know that I would have been different. I would have attracted different circumstances and therefore different outcomes. This marriage was not going to survive a woman who was living a pattern of subconsciously toxic beliefs. No matter what the catalyst for the marriage ending, it was ultimately my responsibility.

The guilt and the failed relationships—from my mother and my father and now from my first marriage—were beginning to pile up. I didn't see it at the time, but I was becoming a prime candidate for a chronic illness.

CHAPTER 20

Making Light of a Difficult Situation

Laughter is therapy for physical pain, emotional pain, and the everyday pain of life.

—Terry Guillemets

I am so aware of how much this disease has affected my life. This physical body that I am inhabiting—I feel that I am a victim of it. The weakness, the fatigue, the pain—oh, the pain—it all sucks! I'm a shell of what I used to be and do for the time being, yet I'm grateful for the times that I can clean, run errands, and play!

Right now, in my mind, I feel confused *much* of the time. I don't use the right words. I feel as if I don't hear people correctly. I tried to learn guitar (and hopefully still will), but I had a hard time understanding what was being taught. This was aside from the hand cramping and swollen knuckle joints, and as I mentioned previously, I literally had bruises on my knuckles from playing piano. I seriously would not have believed it if it hadn't happened to me. There were other reasons that quitting guitar seemed like a good idea at the time. I just miss it.

Anyway, back to the brain fog. I do see the funny in it sometimes. Other times, I feel like a complete weirdo. My humor has been a constant friend throughout my life. I am so thankful for the ability to see things in a different light. I know it can also be a defense mechanism. I am capable of using humor to escape my reality as well, which isn't as healthy. But as long as I'm being completely honest about the situation, having a humorous perspective on a situation during some of the darkest of times has been a release valve.

I said to my daughter, "I think I should take a quick shower in your closet. No, wait. I'll go ahead and take a shower in my closet instead." I would not have noticed what I had said if my daughter had not started laughing. Could this mean that I am going all over town (when I'm not forced to be at home), exchanging words for nonsensical ones and *never* even knowing?

Wow. Sorry, folks, strangers and friends alike. I did find it funny, but it was also sad that my mind couldn't be trusted. And I didn't even really know when I was saying something incorrectly. It was an embarrassing time for me. I knew that I must have sounded drunk or like I was on drugs. I found myself not talking as much in public.

I spent the better part of ten minutes talking to a person that I thought I knew her name. I thought her name was Julie Conrad. During the conversation, she mentioned that she had spoken at length with Julie regarding the issue that we were discussing. I thought *she* was Julie Conrad. Who the hell was I talking to? I still am not positive that I know the name of the person that I was actually speaking with.

Scenario after scenario like this.

I was going to a dinner party at a well-known Japanese restaurant in the area. I went at the right time but to the wrong Japanese restaurant. The dinner party could not be seated until everyone was there, so, of course, all twelve people had to wait on *me* to get across town. The worst part is that I couldn't remember how to get to it. I've lived in this area for over thirty years. It would have been funny, except the people were very angry with me for being late because they could not be seated until everyone was there. There was no room for grace with this set of people. One of them even had an illness, so I thought they would understand. But apparently, brain inflammation from disease was not one of his symptoms, and they had no empathy.

Story after story like this, the same. Some are not funny.

After an hour-and-a-half trip home from receiving an IV treatment, I arrive home ready for a nap. I was so tired. So, I went in and took a nap. I never heard a thing. You'd think I would have. I came outside to pick up my daughter from school, and the car was gone. Where was the car? I thought I was dreaming, and then I looked down the hill and I saw it.

It had rolled down the hill and slammed into a tree. The front end crunched in almost all the way to the windshield. How could I not have heard a crash in my yard? There was $6,500 worth of damage, all because I had not pulled the emergency brake all the way up. Thank God for insurance. I am beyond grateful that no one had been hurt as well. I have to say, my husband at the time was amazing about all of this.

"Accidents happen," he said. "Let's just get it taken care of."

"How long do I bake chicken?" I asked. My husband answered, "Twenty-five minutes."

I went back inside to prepare the baking sheet. Then I went back outside. "How long do I need to bake the chicken again?"

He said, "Twenty-five minutes."

I said, "Okay."

I went back in to put on the barbecue sauce. I was also in so much pain that I could not easily walk across the kitchen and cook anything. By the time the oven was ready and the chicken was prepared, I realized that I still could not remember how long to cook the chicken. I hobbled back out to the porch and apologized for needing to ask again. I assured him that I would write it down this time, and I did, and I pulled out the cooked chicken twenty-five minutes later, perfectly cooked. I'd baked chicken before.

I had trouble with helping my daughter with her first-grade math. I had trouble holding a conversation that made any sense. I still maintained a sense of humor. I sought out funny things to watch and listen to. I completely stopped watching and reading anything that was negative. The news was the first thing to go. There is nothing funny about only hearing about the bad things going on in the planet. I intentionally found funny books and videos. I watched, listened to, or read something funny every day. I wanted to feel myself laugh during the painful times. This one switch in my lifestyle did change things for me. There were at least moments in my days that I could get my mind off the physical symptoms of pain.

CHAPTER 21

Out-of-State Lyme-Literate Doctor

> The greatest gift you can give someone is your
> time, your attention, your love, your concern.
>
> —Joel Osteen

I was so happy! I was able to see one of the best doctors in the country. For us in the Lyme community, he's a bit of a rock star hero. I'd been going to the clinic for two years, but I was seeing him the first time and was quite intimidated. He came in to meet me the first time during my initial visit. I could have chosen to see him, but I was a little ashamed and didn't foresee myself being able to tell him about some of the more private symptoms.

I told him how completely discouraged I'd become. He was very kind. We had a short dialogue about children and about religion. I made jokes because that's what I do when I'm uncomfortable, happy, sad, or crying. He laughed at them, so that was a good thing.

He assured me that he saw this in about one of three patients, that it was a relapse of babesia (a coinfection of Lyme). He said we were going to hit it hard—very aggressively. I told him that I didn't mind suffering; I just didn't want to suffer in vain. He said, "Well put." He also said that he believed that the possible endometriosis was from the Lyme and that he sees saw that a lot.

He was very cool. Soulful eyes. And I could see that he'd been through hell and back in his life. I could see pain and loss in his eyes. I couldn't be sure of all of the whys, only some, but I am thankful for that man. I said to him that I just could not accept this as my life. I just couldn't. I also mentioned that I had to accept it for now. I had to wrap my brain around it because I was lying down looking at the ceiling for much of the time. I felt really desperate for a change in symptoms at this point, but I could not wrap my brain around this being my forever.

He said, "You know, resolve is good. Once you accept it, the fight is over." So even though he didn't seem to be a particularly religious man, I am thankful to God for his amazing journey, courage, and dedication to truth.

Seeing the one woman walking out so slowly, coming up behind her husband, made me tear up more. She was very ill. Everyone in this office was ill to varying degrees. Not to make comparisons, but she was much worse than I was currently. I think it is off-limits to compare ourselves to each other because the symptoms change on a dime. You never really can tell how someone is feeling even if they look better than another with the same disease. My heart felt so much for her—sorrow and loss. I prayed for her recovery.

I could hear the receptionist give the price for the bill. It was $5,575. Many of these visits and medications and treatments were not covered by insurance. This disease carries a hefty price tag. The lady asked how her Christmas was, and she said that she didn't remember most of it. She said that she came down to see her kids open Christmas gifts and went right back up afterward. I'm guessing it was back to bed.

I have since been able to obtain treatment closer to home with a facility that is phenomenal in many areas of practice. People come there from states away as well. Since I have been treating there, I have become much better as well. And I didn't have to travel far to get the help and treatment that I needed. I felt very thankful.

I wish we could change this. I wish there was a cure! What can we do? What can I do? All I can do at this point is share my experience with others.

CHAPTER 22

When Life Becomes Small

Go back and take care of yourself. Your body needs
you, your feelings need you, your perceptions need
you. Your suffering needs you to acknowledge it.
Go home and be there for all these things.

—Thich Nhat Hanh

I was alive even last summer. I got close to some great people, and
then I became symptomatic again to a greater degree. And when
I'm down, I'm really down. I have felt extremely isolated and
helpless. The pain seems ever present. It is muscle pain but also joint
pain. There doesn't seem to be much of a rhyme or reason, and I was
not even able to find a pattern. It may start with abdominal pain or
chest pain. Then comes the finger joint pain and swelling. That's a
first clue that soon it will become knee pain and swelling, then wrist
pain, elbow "fire" (burning-type pain), as well as hip pain on the way
down and even into the toes. It has often felt as if it will never end.

The rest of my dreams and desires for my life have to be put on
hold for now. I'm missing out on some things to preserve some energy.
I know it's off putting sometimes for others. It makes it difficult to
remain close to me. It makes me sad because I don't want to lose
anyone else who is important to me. Truthfully, it looks as if I have
gotten out of many things at a good time. God's timing is perfect.

I only wish I could see it. I know it's true, but I would love to see
it, the arrival, when I can see what it's all been for. I have believed for
so long, and then I fall because "it" still hasn't come. What is "it"?

Fulfillment—the moment when I feel peace and love and know it's all been for this, the moment when I can feel and know that the suffering wasn't in vain. My life has become so small. There seems to be no good reason for all this.

I believe again.

I do.

But I would love some reward now, please.

I am going through another Babesia and possible endometriosis flare, and I was lying in bed. Every finger hurt. I was giving myself permission to stay in bed and in my pajamas. I hope all the right people come into my path today and all the wrong ones stay away. This should become and has become a daily request.

Of course, in my bedroom, I'm likely to only see two people.

So, I pulled up my recorded shows to see some of the forty-four recorded shows, and there were only eleven of them. I yelled for Robert.

"Did you erase my *Twilight Zones*?"

"Yes, we needed space for *The Young and the Restless*."

Seriously, we watch *Y&R*, and he's the one who got me attached.

"What? I had them all recorded in order."

I know I said other things, because I got up and slammed the door. I did that so that I wouldn't say something to be heard that would be cruel, name-cally, and f-bombish.

Then I hit the bed and I cried, sobbing really, because I was so sad that my life had come to this.

During flares, I'm often lying in bed or sitting on the couch, and TV is the only thing I feel I can escape into besides alcohol. Robert and Amazon Prime saved the day, but I was incredibly sad that my life had become so small that I would be completely discouraged by a show being unavailable to watch.

But that's how it is when an illness takes over. Life becomes smaller, and the small things hold a larger-than-life importance. I'm hopeful for the day when my life is large and my illness is not!

I was watching the Hallmark Channel and after *Golden Girls* came a movie about love. This made me a little sad right now. Maybe I was feeling a little lonely. But I felt as if a movie about love made me feel worse.

A friend texted and private messaged to invite us out. I was so thankful and glad. It was such a nice surprise and "now reward."

I learned that when my life became small because of chronic illness, the littlest things mattered. Every good thing matters—a telephone call, a note, a text. Every interaction where someone was kind meant so much more than it ever had before. I thought I had gratitude in my heart prior to the chronic illness. But after it, I definitely did. Even animals coming up to me gave me encouragement and hope. Moments of laughter with my daughter became a lifeline. I began to love life (even if I didn't currently love my own circumstances) in such a great way. I became grateful for the sun and the moon and the stars and the trees. The sunsets meant more, and I loved every single weather condition, not just that which seemed pleasant. The rain and the storm are equally lovely. I had deep gratitude for every season and every condition. I began to see that my condition would also serve its purpose and quite possibly already had. This gratitude, I felt, was a gift.

I began to feel as if this rat race I had been living wasn't life at all. This was. The illness made me stop while the rest of the world kept going. And it hurt like hell that it kept going. And then, in the stillness, the rain still fell and watered the flowers. The flowers still grew. Nature kept going—and maybe for the first time, I would stop to appreciate it. I thank my heart for beating and the sun for rising. And I am thankful that it doesn't need me to direct it. And for a moment, I am at peace.

CHAPTER 23

Chronic Illness Isn't for the Faint of Heart

> You're going into a season where you're about to experience breakthrough after breakthrough because what you went through didn't break you.
>
> —Kimberly Jones Pothier

I've come close to the point where it's harder to write because the feelings are so strong and so deep that the thought of anyone knowing them at this time seems scary. The day-to-day interactions with people are different after acquiring an illness than they were before I became ill.

Some people with this disease are intensely bothered by it when unknowing people state that they look healthy. I personally *love* this. Someone with this illness only looks healthy for a while. Inevitably, it rips your body apart. There was a time that I looked sick, and sometimes still, even as I am looking better and better because I'm still working on it, I look like crap! So, I love to hear that I look great or well or not sick. I'm so fine with it! And thank you!

One of the favorite questions that I used to get from my husband and friends that really care about how I'm doing is "What hurts right now?" I like this question because usually it comes when I look like I'm well and happy but I tell them I'm in terrible pain. Not many people get the truth from me about the daily realities of this disease.

That isn't because I don't want to tell people, but it's because it is so difficult to explain. It's also pretty depressing, so I don't put others through it often. I put on a pretty good show. No one would ever know that *all* of that is going on at that time because I seem so fine. Answering this question gives an accurate picture of this sometimes invisible illness. I tell them that I smile and laugh and love in spite of the pain, not because it isn't there.

I'm playing a little game right now, because tonight, everyone saw a happy-go-lucky version of myself (which is the real me at heart). "What hurts right now?" Even right now, my feet are tingling, my hands tingle off and on, my hands also burn, I have pain in my ulna, the back of my head, and the left side of my face, and my tongue was even tingling—and that is one strange sensation. The joint pain is amazingly present, more so at night but also in the day. Everything seems so much worse at night.

Right now, there is incredible pain on the right side under my rib cage. I feel intuitively that this comes from my liver. It has been the catchall of four *full* years of heavy antibiotics, antimalarials, and antiviral medications and then many follow-up years with off-and-on medications. This pain is amplified right now by the Epstein-Barr virus. The liver pain sometimes makes me feel as if I'm going to pass out. And let's not even get started on the hip pain.

I've taken Xylitol, Lactoferrin, Ceftin, and Septra. All this will be repeated later. I will also need to take liquid iron, vitamins A, C, D, and E, CoQ10 (only when not on Mepron), and fish oil—and this is a light day. Yesterday was Mepron, Lactoferrin, Xylitol, Artemisia, Enula, Ceftin, and Septra, along with the supplements. This was done twice this day, as it will be again tomorrow.

This isn't even the heaviest of days where I do all this, plus Flagyl and Diflucan. How has my body been doing this for so long? Why isn't it done yet? How much longer?

Sadly, some have done this for as long as seventy to nine years before remission.

I wish I could yell at this illness. "Get out, organisms, bacteria, fungi, viruses, and parasites—*out of my body*. Please." My body and my mind are so tired right now. I honestly just wish it was over with. I'm sure many battling any chronic illness feel this way.

The next day, and nothing much has changed. The health check-in—headache, fever, finger ache, arm pain, joint pain, hip pain, pelvic pain, abdominal pain. Oh, and I had something removed in my uterus in January 2016. I had never actually heard a doctor say this before. During the ultrasound, he moved the camera around, and he asked the nurse, "What is that?" He stopped and looked at her and said, "Do you see that? What is that?" Okay, so, surgery scheduled. But it doesn't incite a great feeling when surgery is needed because they don't know what is inside your uterus.

It ended up being polyps, fibroids, and debris. Yes. He said there was *debris* in my uterus. It sounded as if there had been a car accident in there, but I did get some relief after this surgery.

I'm tired of being afraid in the wee hours of the morning. Right now, I'm a little pissed about it. I'm pissed that I'm in such a great deal of pain, and although I have well-meaning doctors, they can't seem to cure me. This road is too hard, and I have done everything I have been directed to do. It seems that, even though I have had the best of the best with respect to doctors and my medical team, I am still floundering. I am told this is part of the process and that I will still recover. Healing is not linear, and I will have moments of two steps forward and three steps back, but I am out of steam.

I am thankful for good doctors and simply weary of fear. So, even though I'm in pain, unhappy about my situation, and lonely, I choose to drink in every moment of beauty and love wherever I cross their path. I'm tired of being tired. I'm tired of regretting my decisions. I'm tired of being afraid that I'm going to die. I'm tired of being sick. I choose to surrender to God and see what happens next.

I honestly felt like I might die soon. I realized I was in full-blown relapse. I have to say, I've had small moments of doubt that I would get well, but mostly, I have honest to God believed that I would get better. Since this relapse, I am having a difficult time believing it. I am in such pain. I can feel everything in my body swelling. I'm actually afraid now. God, am I going to die?

At this point, I realize I have been treating this illness with a pharmacy full of medications. I became about 60 percent better and then relapsed. What was going on here? Why was I getting worse again? Why did some people get well and some did not? Even though I wanted to give up, I now had something else to try for. I was going to try some new things. I had decided that part of this had to be the emotional pain and trauma I had suffered many years ago that kept me in this space. I was in an ongoing state of physical disease because my emotions were still not healed from the trauma of abuse and emotional wounds I had suffered. It was time to address the whole person now.

I began to look into meditation, self-hypnosis, and energy medicine. And what I found there was extraordinary. I have included some resources in the back of this book that helped me when I began this part of the chronic illness journey. I began to meditate daily, and it did *not* come naturally, but it was amazing. I would even play meditation and hypnosis YouTube videos overnight while I was asleep. I began learning about breathing exercises and how important it is to begin connecting with your body through breathing and other physical exercises. Sometimes you cannot reason your way through trauma and pain; only by connecting to your highest self can you process these old ways of thinking and believing. It became clear that, on some level, I had to change my hardwired negative and self-sabotaging beliefs. It was subconscious beliefs from the trauma and abuse that were keeping me ill. I had no doubt.

CHAPTER 24

Anxiety

Fear is what blinds us to the real danger of life. In fact, fear itself is the greatest danger that the human body faces. It is fear and guilt that bring about disease and failure in every area of our lives. We could take the same protective actions out of love rather than out of fear.

—David R. Hawkins, M.D., Ph.D

The worst lies are the ones we tell ourselves. The worst verbal abuse comes from our own tongue. The most negative influence is the devil on our own shoulder. The cruelest judge is the one staring back in the mirror. The person really withholding the love you need is you. No one will ever out-do you at your own mind-games. You must stop doing this to yourself!

—Bryant McGill

I'm pretty insecure. Pretty guilty feeling for—well, for everything. But that makes no difference now. Guilt is a close cousin to shame, and they are so closely intertwined that they're almost indiscernible. I'm dreadfully tired of both.

Anxiety is a rude nag. It incessantly rides me about everything. The extrovert (me, in this case) craves social interactions; it needs them and doesn't do well for long without them. Extroverts actually *thrive* on interactions with other people and gain energy when they are. But extroverts with anxiety—well, that's a whole different animal. If you have an anxious extrovert who is also guilt ridden and shame based, it always feels like crazy time. I had some anxiety prior to the illness, but after Lyme disease, it became unmanageable. The brain is actually inflamed along with the rest of the body. I know that this is part of the reason everything was magnified, but having all my insecurities and fears magnified seemed difficult to overcome.

There is not a single interaction that doesn't leave me in a ruminative state for days, berating myself and usually someone else too. This is an exhausting existence. What is the salve for this? Is there a cure for worry?

Well, if you have Lyme disease, you cannot help it. Treatment will certainly improve these conditions, but if you've struggled with this all your life, one of the cures is actually solitude. I know this seems simplistic and possibly counterintuitive, but spending a lot of time alone gives you the gift of breaking out of the fear of being alone. Being alone is actually an antidote to loneliness. It seems counterintuitive, but it's absolutely true. I was given an opportunity here to do the work of addressing these ghosts of fear and panic that had followed me all my life. Because it was magnified, I could no longer avoid it. The many hours that I spent alone and isolating myself ended up being some of the most healing time I had ever spent. And after months and months of intentional time every day alone, I began to love it. I don't think I have been afraid of time alone since. It actually made my time of fellowship with friends and family richer too. This too was a gift, but I didn't see it that way until much later.

It also helps you to know yourself. When you know yourself, you begin to accept yourself. When you accept yourself, you can and will see that you are worthy of the love that you've been trying to find out there. What we've been looking for out there is really in here and has been all along. You will love yourself with a knowing that this has been what is missing. You are what you have been missing.

Here's the truth: people aren't thinking about you nearly as much as you are thinking about yourself. You might pick out a few sentences that someone else says and remember those and ruminate over them, but that is only—I repeat, *only*—because it either offended you (hurt feelings) or made you feel fantastic (fed the ego).

I want to be a better person, a nicer person, a better friend.

So now I feel like I am not as judgmental as I once was when people would talk about all their suffering. I didn't want to hear it. I thought they were being negative, that maybe they were attention seeking, maybe they liked the attention that they were getting from being ill. I did think that there were some people who, given the choice to be well or ill, would choose to be ill.

Now I know that was foolish. I always saw chronically ill people like I saw my mother. She had mental illness before cancer took her life at fifty-nine. She had access to meds that could have stabilized her, and she wouldn't take them. I saw that as her fault. That too was ignorance. Now I know this, because being afraid to take those medications was part of that illness. My grandmother was physically ill with COPD and constantly complained. Now I know that it wasn't merely judgment. It was also fear.

Now I don't see chronically sick patients as I once did. Now I know that we don't *want* to be sick. We would prefer to not have the kind of attention that we have been receiving. We are tired of being called crazy. We are tired of hurting and herxing and crying. We are tired of being tired, and we don't want to be sick. We want to be healed. We want a cure! We want, at the very least, not to have the effing validity of the disease in our bodies questioned.

I have been crying, praying, popping, and pooping pills, and smoking weed in order to get some relief. I have cried in a tub in the middle of the night, vomited, and laid on a couch and on the floor while weeping. I suffered hour after hour, month after month, and now even year after year. Yes, now I am one of them. I am with those who suffer with chronic illness. But no stone will be left unturned. There is a way out of this. There has to be.

My daughter and I went to a neighbor's house for a playdate. As soon as I took my coat off, a CMA from my doctor's office called. I gave them the information and became emotional because the guy said that I had to be my own advocate. There were times that I felt as if I were my only advocate. I nearly yelled, which was barely above a whisper for me. I vehemently spat out that I had asked this same question now four times and that everyone had seemed to avoid it. I was wondering if there was a possibility that the new tick bite had caused this relapse.

I got off of the phone and sat down with my neighbor. I cried right there, weeping really. And she held me. It really was so sweet of her. I felt like so much emotionally pent-up pain was coming out. And there was a loud thump a few minutes later, and my daughter started crying. She had fallen and gotten a pretty quick bruise on her shin. I comforted her and she went to watch a show.

"The Paiges come over to the neighbors just to cry." We left soon after that, to which my daughter said, "That was the worst play date I've ever had."

Yep, she is right, I thought.

My hands are important to me. I love playing the piano. I can also play flute and clarinet. I was even learning the guitar. Even now, typing this is causing me to notice the discomfort in my hands.

I took for granted how amazing it was to be able to count on them. They'd pick up things, move things, play with things, hold things and love people, and create things. It is scary and sad to have them hurt so much! It is scary to lose the ability to do—well, anything. Thank You, God, for the full use of my hands. I say thank You before I see the manifestation of my healing. It is what we are told to do, claim what isn't as if it were. And it is a sacrifice of thanksgiving and a sacrifice of praise.

I'm afraid. I don't want to be afraid. I've always been afraid of almost everything, but now, I'm sure that I have been afraid 365 days a year about something. I was taught to be afraid of illness, of food, of people, of most everything in life. This has left me in a state of near-constant anxiety. If the pain continues, I feel as though I'll have to give up the fight. I don't know if it's possible, though, for me to give up on something. I tend to hold on to something until it has ruined me. I will hold onto a person, goal, or hope until it has wrecked me.

In the beginning of this illness, after the recurring sinus infections came the respiratory infections. I then experienced knee pain, followed by back pain. The excruciating back pain felt like tearing, burning, aching—like a knife being plunged into it and then twisted turned sideways and then sliced through from one side to the other after it had been held over a fire for many hours. I was truly afraid. I had never had such agonizing pain before this.

I first thought that I had hurt myself, that I had pulled or torn a muscle. I was diagnosed with a pinched nerve and carpal tunnel because by the time I could get in to see the neurologist, my arm was going to sleep. The tingling started on one side, and then the other side. My leg began to hurt and then tingle. Then my foot began to tingle, then feel numb. Soon after came the other side, the leg and foot. It was pleural neuropathy. Then my hands started to tingle, and my arm became tingly. When I would wake up, I could not feel my arm and hand. They were completely numb. This was peripheral neuropathy.

I began dropping things. I was tripping. I was slurring my words. I began choking on my food, and sometimes I would choke just from my saliva. I couldn't remember words for things, so I would often stop in the middle of sentences. I once forgot where I was. I reassured myself, "Calm down. Look at the bags. Where do the bags say you are?"

"Lowes."

"Okay! Now, which way to go home."

This was the moment that I knew something was very wrong. Until this point, others had me thinking and believing that it was anxiety or all in my head. I was not merely afraid at this point. I felt sheer terror. I was losing complete control of my physical body. I also was losing control over my own mind, but I was aware that I was losing these abilities.

The left side of my face began to tingle, then the back of my head, and then my tongue. I began to choke on my own spit, and it was difficult to swallow. There were four ER visits. One of my ER visits turned into an admission with the virus previously mentioned in chapter 2. One visit, I was sent to a neurologist because the doctor believed that I had an autoimmune illness—his top belief was that it was multiple sclerosis. After one of the visits, I was sent home with a diagnosis of a reaction to pain medication. One sent me to an orthopedic surgeon, and the last believed it was uncontrolled anxiety. I lost twenty-one pounds in nine weeks, and by this time, I was losing about three pounds every five days. I felt sheer terror. I was horrified and terrified. I was really afraid that I was dying. And I was stricken with an awareness that I had not yet really lived. I had experienced some amazing moments, but I had not lived life to the fullest, and I was going to leave this world not having lived life to the fullest. This was my greatest fear and my greatest regret. I was trapped in my body with this pain and tingling and numbness. My body and life were literally falling apart, with a new symptom every few days and then, seemingly, every day.

The heart palpitations began. The headaches and the weird electrical pulses would plague me, and they were so very odd. Everything was literally going haywire. I was a central nervous system and autonomic nervous system nightmare. I was having daily panic attacks. The pain that was shooting into my feet and toes felt like bee stings.

I was so cold—all the time! I wore long-sleeve shirts in 95-degree weather. My feet were so cold that I remember driving from Greensboro to Winston-Salem between doctors' appointments and having to stop at my condo and warm my feet with a heating pad. I felt as if I were experiencing hypothermia. I would shiver, and my teeth would chatter. I don't know if there was any body part that remained unaffected by this horrible disease! What a nightmare! There was a decent to probable chance that I was going to die from this. But I had not yet discovered what it was. I was going to doctor after doctor to find out.

I remembered the tick bite and my friend whom I had met three years prior. She had to learn to walk again after this disease and its coinfections had ravaged her body. I called her, and she urged me to see a certain the same prior Lyme-literate infectious disease doctor that I mentioned previously (most infectious disease doctors will tell you that there is no such thing as chronic Lyme disease, but they are committing medical malpractice by telling patients this as a truth). Usually, *infectious disease* and *Lyme literate* are oxymorons, but I'm going out on a limb by saying they should go hand in hand. In one hundred years, the denial of the severity of this illness will be known as a huge medical travesty, a complete medical and moral failure.

I told her that I couldn't imagine seeing someone five states away and that it would be so expensive for the first visit. I was separated at the time, and it was his money that I was spending, so I would go to one closer to home. She was the doctor of this woman's daughter whom I had met in an Al-Anon meeting.

She was going to an Al-Anon support group for her daughter's Lyme disease. She had severe chronic Lyme disease. She gave me the name of the "local" doctor who could help me. She was two hours away. I was also given the name of someone a bit more local. Because I knew someone who was friends with the office manager, I was able to get in within three weeks instead of two months, so I kept both appointments. I was diagnosed with Lyme disease twice—within one week of each other. I could no longer deny this diagnosis.

I was a mess. I wasn't sleeping because of the pain. I wasn't sleeping, because insomnia is another gift that this disease has to offer. Every day, and sometimes several times a day, there was a fresh new hell. The pain was constant in my back. But the other pain would migrate. It might be in my arm. Then it would dissipate, only to show up in my side or legs.

There were muscle spasms. I could sit and watch my arm or some areas of my leg jump and twitch. It was visible to anyone who would be watching. Usually, during this time, I would be alone because there wasn't much that I could do. My daughter was in kindergarten at the time. I did the best I could do to pick up my daughter from school and play with her. I would have to set several alarms so I would remember to go and get her and when. It was awful.

Before the diagnosis, I was separated from my husband for about six weeks and was attempting this alone. Before returning home, though, I was having such severe panic attacks that I would call him to come over because I was afraid and tired, oh so tired. The disease was wreaking havoc on my autonomic nervous system as well as my central nervous system. This was apparently the reason for the repeated panic attacks.

One night (and this was one of the last I was alone with Katherine with this illness), I almost fainted. I had a weird pain in my head. During the last part before diagnosis, I had this caved-in feeling to the left side of my head. The tunnel vision began, and I could barely breathe. My daughter was in the bed asleep. I was so scared. I couldn't stand up well because my vision had narrowed and I felt so weak, so I crawled to my neighbor's across the hall and knocked on the door from the floor. They opened and called 911. The female stranger came across the hallway to my condo and watched my child until I returned home in a cab at four o'clock in the morning. This turned out to be a reaction to one of pain medications, which had not controlled the pain. I was losing it.

I was grateful that she came, but it became clear that I was not going to be able to continue the way things were. I knew that I could no longer take care of my daughter alone. Even I, her own mother, couldn't be trusted to care for her, my beautiful, wonderful, innocent daughter. So I returned home to my husband. We decided that under the circumstances, she needed us both together. I love her more than any other person on this planet, and I was not able to raise her. This couldn't be happening, not to me, not after everything that I had been through. And not to her. She didn't deserve this. She needed me. I needed to live.

CHAPTER 25

Darker Times

I will not die; instead, I will live to tell
what the LORD has done.

—Psalm 118:17 (NLT)

This pain made me wish I would die. But no, I had to live. How could I die if I had to? What if the pain never went away? Seven years later, the pain is still here, and I have ordered a book that tells me how to kill myself.

> Most of my HIV patients used to die ... now most don't ... some still do, of course. My Lyme patients, the sickest ones, want to die but they can't. THAT'S RIGHT, they want to die but they can't.
> —Dr. Joseph G. Jemsek, MD, FACP

I am only trying to be honest about how amazingly and surprisingly awful this pain can be. It's like nothing I've ever known. And yet, I know it now, every minute of every day. I'm done. I so wanted something in my life to be positive and equally surprising and amazing but good-news worthy and positive and happy. I wanted to feel as though I had succeeded at something, as though I had contributed something greater than myself to the world, as though I had achieved greatness, happiness, or fulfillment, even if it was merely within myself.

Don't get me wrong. I have an amazing, beautiful, perfect daughter. I could not ask for more from a daughter. I've had some cool things happen. I thank God, if He is real, for that. I want more of that good feeling. I have a lot of money. Who the hell cares about money? I can't get rid of the pain. I would trade it all to be well and out of this trap.

At this time, I truly feel as though it would be better if I were gone. Suicide is not a coward's way out, and it is not for the weak, it is so scary to figure this out. But I honestly think that leaving everyone behind is better than continuing to suffer in front of everyone, day after day and year after year. Suicide is the leading cause of death of those with Lyme disease. I wondered if I would become another suicide statistic. This is agony. I can feel it now. I will not get better. *What a horrible existence that You insisted that I keep going with. Even you can't keep me here. I will kill myself,* I heard my thoughts say.

Only to Katherine am I truly sorry. To everyone else, you've caused this also.

There are some really dark days with this illness and with depression. There are some days when ending it all seems like the only way out. Most won't write on this subject. I have become so desperate that I researched ways to end it that would not leave myself and my family in complete shambles. This sounds strange to hear and now even to say. Now that I've found some space from the pain, I know how far down the slippery slide I must have been.

I even considered hiring a hitman. Ha! Really, a hitman. *For myself.* It's really not a bad idea. And no, those who commit suicide *do not go to hell*! Those who perpetuate this lie are fearful and want to control the behavior of others. Those who say victims of suicide are cowards are *wrong*! Facing a decision like this and planning for it is one of the bravest things a person can do. Deciding to end a life takes more bravery than any act I can imagine. My lack of bravery is one of the reasons I did not, even at my worst times, give in to the temptation to take my own.

I do think suicide should never be taken lightly. I do believe, however, that the terminally ill should have an option to get help if they are in a perpetual state of suffering. Most importantly, I simply do not think that people should judge those with loved ones who have attempted or ultimately committed suicide. I honestly believe that we should show Grace to those who are struggling, especially if we have not fought the same battles. Perhaps we should simply be thankful that we have not had to walk in their shoes.

I want to talk about what happened to me when I came close to death. I am not one of those people who had a near-death experience. There are many amazing people who have died and returned. They have told of the unexplainable and extraordinary acceptance and unconditional love they felt upon crossing over. I have included some book titles of their accounts at the end of this book. I would strongly recommend that anyone who has a fear of dying read some of these books.

At the beginning of this illness and before the diagnosis, I felt trepidation at the thought of what alien might be taking over my body as faculties were seemingly being stripped from me almost daily. As it was becoming more and more difficult to walk and to do much of any useful thing, I decided that if my end was approaching, I wanted to be at the beach. My family made allowances for me, and I drove to the beach alone. This was no easy feat, since I was in constant pain and could barely stand up straight, much less carry luggage, walk, and drive on my own. But I honestly thought this might be one of the last opportunities to drive and to take a trip like this. It was important that I go.

Once I arrived, I took a lot of nerve pain medications and sat on the balcony. I talked to a few loved ones on the phone, had some wine, and took in the views as if it might be the last time I would see the ocean in this way. I so loved it here. I don't remember much else about that night.

I was in severe pain and took a lot of medication so I could walk out to the beach. In my mind, I was going to walk on the beach, possibly for the last time. I don't mean to sound so dramatic. But at this time in my experience, death was a real possibility. I had lost twenty-one pounds in nine weeks. I had done CT scans, MRI scans, an endoscopy, a colonoscopy, and a spinal tap. Vials and vials of blood had been drawn, everyone could see that I was wasting away, and no one could yet tell what was happening to me. Those who have been devastated by this disease know that this is an experience that some and maybe many of us have: the fear of death staring us in the face.

I was ramped up on pain medications, so I was determined to walk. As I walked, I was touched by the beauty of the ocean, the beach, and the amazing day. I was in love with all of it, and I was sad to feel the loss of my abilities. But for now, I could appreciate all my senses in a way I had not appreciated quite as much before. I could see the amazing ocean. I could smell the salt air. I could hear the seagulls and the waves of the ocean crashing onto the sand. I could hear the sounds of people talking and children laughing. I could feel the sand in my toes and the water running over my feet. And for those moments, I was thankful.

I had not walked far. Getting down to the beach from the hotel was the longest part of my walk, but it felt so good to walk this much. On the way back to the hotel, which might as well have been on the moon, I got a surge of energy. And that's what it was—energy, pure positive energy. I began walking faster and faster, then began running. It was a short burst, but it was beautiful, and it was lovely!

I paid for this dearly when I returned to the room. I collapsed in pain and severe exhaustion. I lay on the bed looking up at the ceiling. I felt as if I'd released my spirit to God. I said out loud that I wanted God to take me from this pain and hold me in His unconditional light and love, where I could be restored and loved for eternity. That sounded like bliss right now, and leaving it all behind was a small price to pay for a body riddled with physical and emotional pain.

That was the first time that I had not felt afraid and actually felt relief. I could go home now.

There was one other moment. This moment, however, was when I thought it was entirely possible. It was during the ER visit (one of many) that I had mentioned in the beginning of the book.

I was so sick that I could barely walk across the floor. I could barely lift my head up, as the pressure in my head was narrowing my vision. I couldn't focus on anything because the room was swaying and slightly spinning. It felt as though someone with large hands was cupping my ears, squeezing my head tightly and shading my eyes so that everything had an eerie greenish or yellowish color to it. I was in the hospital bed, and I couldn't lift my head up much because it all felt so strange. Every time I tried, I would get so queasy, and I didn't want to begin throwing up again.

I was terrified! I was afraid of leaving my family. I was fully convinced that I was dying. I didn't know how Katherine would make it without me. I loved her so much and wanted to raise her. I wasn't so afraid of leaving my husband, as I knew he would be fine. If anything, I carried so much guilt for being sick that I believed it may be a relief not to have me as a burden. But I was afraid for myself. I was angry at not having experienced *all* of the special things that I had hoped to before I left this planet.

I was clawing emotionally at life. I was resisting and tormented by the threat of dying from this virus and ultimately from Lyme disease. But this is the thing. This is the *beautiful* thing. When I released the resistance, when I gave in to the possibility of dying and leaving the world behind, the strangest thing happened. I gave in, and the peace of God came over me in an instant. It was immediate! As soon as I surrendered everything to God, I was flooded with peace. I knew that it didn't matter if I lived or died. I knew that this form was merely the physical form of my eternal being. I knew that my daughter would be fine, even well. I knew everything was going to be okay. I even knew that I was going to be okay.

At that moment, I realized dying is not the worst thing that could happen to me, or anyone. I realized that we don't die; we only change form. And I realized I could feel the peace of God over the fear of death from now on, for the rest of my physical life in this incarnation as me. And of course, I did not die.

CHAPTER 26

My Biggest Regrets

> Regardless of how much you judge yourself for
> your past, know that the road you took was
> exactly the one you needed to take to give you
> the experiences and knowledge you have now.
>
> —James Blanchard Cisneros

I have been really hard on myself my entire life. I judged myself harshly and expected to be able to keep going strong after all of the self-criticism. I tried to hate myself into loving myself, and that does not work. Then came mistakes that were so big, so terrible, that I could not forgive myself. And they are the reasons I became and stayed ill for so long. Sometimes it feels as if the loneliness alone might kill me. I know it won't, because it's been much worse than it is now. Even as a child, the loneliness was ever present. If I could even put words to the heaviness of this feeling, it would be soul-sucking anguish. A void. Me-less. And yet, I'm still here. Why am I still here?

I feel as if I spend so much time alone. The illness is only a part of that. I've felt it before, so much so that going from person to person became necessary. For a while, I would be fulfilled, then become dissatisfied. It wasn't quick; sometimes it could take years, but usually I was not bored, more like unfulfilled. I would think that it just must not be the right person for me. I kept thinking that if I could just find that one right person, I would be happy, fulfilled.

I dated a lot but slept with only two people. That doesn't make me innocent though.

I think I always felt I was with the wrong person, so I justified changing into a different person even while I was married.

When I knew John was wrong, I went to Robert. When I felt Robert was wrong, I went to someone else. I told myself that I really loved this person so that I could feel okay about cheating. I didn't sleep with him, but did so much that it was close.

I wasn't sad at all when I was caught, and I didn't talk to him again. Of course, I was sad for my husband and the families involved, even though I felt as though I had been so alone that it shouldn't have been a big surprise to anyone. It was tough. I wasn't sad when he didn't reach out. I certainly didn't reach out to him. His big explanation to my husband was, "I didn't fuck your wife, Robert."

But the damage was done—to my family, to Robert's boys, to his ex-wife, to his parents, even to the dog trainer. Yes, Robert told everyone. *Everyone.* Not everyone knew right away, but when I separated from him a year and a half later, he continued to tell everyone. I was shamed in every way. He was pissed, and he was hurt, so I lied about the extent of the affair. I did so because he could be violent, and I was very afraid. Plus, I didn't want to hurt him more than I already had with details of the extent of the affair.

When he found out the whole truth, that I had been meeting him for months and more dirty details about the acts themselves (which, of course, the other guy was forced to tell), he hit me so hard in the cheekbone and ear with the bony part of his arm that his arm turned green, then developed a greenish-black bruise. I had trouble hearing for a couple of days. I told only those closest to me. I was not symptomatic yet when this happened. It would be a few months before the disease would catch up with me.

My daughter heard me scream as I fell on the bed and came running to see if I was okay. I was so stunned that I said it out loud, "Daddy hit me, but I'm okay." I don't think I would have said that to my four-year-old daughter if I had my wits about me. I am still shocked that it didn't even leave a bruise. It hurt so much, and it was so hard that I didn't know if he had broken my cheekbone or his arm. I wasn't entirely positive that I'd hear the same again.

I'm sure some out there would say that I deserved it. They understand the crime of passion. For years, I felt I deserved it too. But now I know differently. I could have slept with twelve men and still would not have deserved to have anyone put his hands on me—*ever*.

People don't have to stay together. If they hurt each, they no longer have to stay in that relationship. I'm not in any way saying that it is okay to continue a cheating relationship, and I will not ever do that to myself or another living being. The pain to everyone is too great, even to the cheater, believe it or not.

I am only saying that we do not own each other and that most people don't go around cheating on each other (although there are some). I went to counseling after this, as I have many times in my life. I wondered if this cheater was just who I was, and I was helped to see that, no, I was not a serial cheater. I simply had terrible patterns. Instead of leaving a relationship and being alone, I would get into something else. I did not do that when I left him the last time. I was alone. And it felt as if I had at least done that right and finally begun to unravel these broken and flawed patterns. This time, I was breaking generational curses.

I didn't just hurt myself and my marriage. I also acquired Lyme disease because I went to the mountains with a man that I thought I was in love with. But still, I was cheating, and that wasn't my husband. I didn't know until that evening. I saw the tick on my thigh when I was at my daughter's recital. It had only been there about five or six hours (not the thirty-six hours that the CDC website states that a tick must be there in order to transfer the disease). I worried for several days, but since the bull's-eye rash and flu-like symptoms didn't come, I figured I was fine. I was far from fine, but I wouldn't know that until about a month's later. In hindsight, I started manifesting signs about four months later.

Was this a punishment for having the affairs? Was this an instant karma? Some might say yes. I even thought so for a while. I thought I deserved to be sick. I even asked for it because Robert began to treat me worse and worse, and my self-esteem got lower and lower. I simply saw no way out. I guess he too thought that he had the right. I'm sure I would have punished him too had the situation been reversed, but thinking back, it may or may not have been on a smaller scale.

I felt as though I had been punished twice now. I had tried to fix our marriage for a long time, and Robert had addiction issues with alcohol and weed. He even took our three-year-old to buy it once. The whole SUV smelled like it. I could smell it from the street. I begged him to stop drinking as much, as he was abusive when he was drunk. When I said he had a problem, he made fun of me. I felt as though I were being punished. And then I was caught for trying to find some kind of love, for cheating, and then I was punished again with a disease that gave me the worst pain I could imagine.

I don't know if I believe in karma, though. I say that as if it were instant karma, because the accurate definition for karma is "consequences received in the next life for actions in this one." Most do not use the definition correctly. I'm speaking purely in terms of instant karma. Although some may say I had it coming, I say that if karma were true, I would have gotten all of the emotional good that I had given coming to me as well. I have gotten a lot of great things and people though. I think getting this disease as a punishment would have been overkill. I don't think anyone could ever *deserve* this kind of pain. I should have had a lot more emotional kindness and love coming to me, both in my childhood and in my adult life. The karmic scales did not seem balanced.

Children don't deserve abuse, so I don't believe in instant karma. Of course, I'm supposing that the counterargument of that: that we reap things from our past lives. That is the correct use of the word anyway. I still don't buy that any child deserves any cruelty, whether or not it is payment for past lives. There is no justice in that. In fact, if that is a thing, it serves only to continue the patterns of abuse and goes against what karma promotes anyway, which is growth and lasting change to the self and to the planet.

I thought we were supposed to learn to become better people, not beaten down by mistakes until there is nothing left. I believe I had, and maybe have, a lot more good coming my way. I believe that I deserve much more good in my life, body, mind, and spirit.

I don't believe that I got punished for trying to find love, even though it hurt a lot of people twice. I think the consequences of those actions are enough punishment.

I was *so* lonely. I can explain both times and try to justify them. I had convinced myself that I couldn't leave and that to get love, I had to find it outside the marriage—just one of many misguided judgments. I simply thought I had chosen poorly again, had not found the right one, and that this new one, that new one, whichever new one, would be the one. The problem with that is that it always ensures that my happiness is *out there*. It's always in someone else's hands.

It never really occurred to me that I was the one responsible for this pattern. That I was causing it. That neither of those marriages was going to work right out of the gate. Or that maybe I could have attracted healing and a different outcome had I done the work while I was in the relationship. The wounds from past sexual and emotional trauma had not been healed prior to latching myself onto another person. Therefore, these relationships may have been doomed from the start. I put it this way because I do not know what is next for me. I do not know if I will try the marriage thing again or just have fulfilling relationships with myself and others along the way. But I do know that I have done the work.

The judgment I had toward myself about my patterns was immense, and I needed mercy. I needed it from others' judgments as well. But I really needed to give myself grace. I was looking for love in all the wrong ways, and I was trapped in flawed thinking. And now I understand that the failed relationships were not my fault. They were my responsibility, but they weren't my fault. But that means they weren't anyone else's fault, either. I understand now that we were all simply repeating our patterns without much consciousness. I am on good terms with both of these men. I think, on some level, we have all just forgiven each other. Or at least I hope so. I know I feel only love. But now I feel love for myself most of all. And it's about time.

CHAPTER 27

The Good Days—There Are Some

The goal is progress, not perfection.

—Becky Voliser

Dr. Wayne Dyer said to be on the lookout for the opportunity to say to yourself, "I feel good." I intend to attract more of this good feeling, and I intend to give it away to any and all in need of it.

There were many times when things were at their worst and I remained mostly in the house, day after day. I was either in bed or on the couch, hour after hour, taking two and sometimes three baths per day to control the pain. I had fear. When the minutes turn into hours, days, weeks, months, and then years, I had some doubt, sometimes a lot of doubt. The months turned into years, and my relapses caused terror and despair.

But still …

When the pain was under control and I could distract myself, I could feel normal, I could feel well for a short time, and I wanted to keep feeling like that.

I feel *good,* and I want to keep feeling like that.

I should mention that before the relapse, I was off of *all* nerve-pain meds, off all regular antiinflammatories, even off Cymbalta (used for nerve pain), which also helped with anxiety and depression.

I was so close …

I felt normalcy, not perfection but normalcy. And I kept fighting for perfection. But right now, these four to six hours will be wonderful. Right now is wonderful. All I have is *now*. All any of us have is now. I feel good!

It's nice when there is a break in the clouds. Sometimes, there is a ray of hope, deep in your soul. Sometimes, a person puts it there. Sometimes, there's a break in the normal rift. Sometimes, your dream comes true. Whatever it is, when it happens, it breathes life back into your soul and makes everything else that seemed hopeless now seem possible.

I've noticed that it requires honesty. A break in the clouds makes me admit just how lifeless I have felt. I now realize that whether or not I should be happy with all I have, I am not. It was hard to understand this at first because I thought the illness made me feel unhappy. I am quite unhappy during a flare.

But before that, before I got sick, there was always something I was unhappy about. I tried to cover it up, to distract myself. I tried to achieve more so that I could ignore or deal with the loneliness I felt inside. During my flare ups, I tried again to cover it and ignore the pain and loneliness. Cover it up. Fill it up.

I'm sure drinking again had something to do with the relapse. It wasn't occasional. It was daily. Again, I wasn't getting drunk all of the time, but it was terrible for my body. It is so important to have a healthy relationship with food and drink of all kinds. I don't drink anymore to fill a void. I know that I used to be trying just to avoid feeling emptiness. Mostly, I don't drink at all anymore.

I just wanted to kill the loneliness and the fear.

I needed to find peace. I must make a change, because I must find peace. There was none inside me. I was utterly and undoubtedly clinically depressed. Growth, change, and salvation come from being honest with yourself about where you truly are in your life. I was completely lost.

CHAPTER 28

Last Thought on Mortality

I am always saddened by the death of a good person.
It is from this sadness that a feeling of gratitude
emerges. I feel honored to have known them and
blessed that their passing serves as a reminder to me
that my time on this beautiful earth is limited and
that I should seize the opportunity I have to forgive,
share, explore, and love. I can think of no greater
way to honor the deceased than to live this way.

—Steve Maraboli

The outer manifestation of this illness in my life is a direct reflection of the state of my heart, soul, emotions, and mind. I have continued to drag myself through life, ignoring the pain of a repeatedly broken heart. I was certain that if I could just attain the right person, place, or thing, it would make up for the abuse and loss suffered from childhood and right on through to adulthood, that it would all be fine.

When I was first ill, I was standing, although barely able to, at the kitchen window watching my husband play in the yard with our daughter. I was heartbroken at where I was and where I wasn't. I still did not know what was wrong and was literally losing three pounds a week and becoming feeble. I was in severe pain, and I was crying. A voice said to me in my mind, *This is how much pain you've been in your entire life. This is how you've always felt on the inside and you were never going to listen.*

The fear associated with this illness is insidious, hideous, atrocious, terrifying, and evil. I have heard from and read about many Lyme disease patients. I am one. In the early days of this disease presenting itself, I had recently been through a couple of traumas. A high school friend had died of cancer. I was thirty-five, so this was huge. I hadn't spoken with him since graduation, but we had been in concert band and orchestra together. In fact, we went to the prom together. We weren't a couple; we were in a small group of couples.

We would have crossed paths that very fall because our kids went to school together (and still do). I met his wife that same fall after the summer that he died. His death was traumatizing. Reading of the last days of his journey was petrifying. He began chemo and soon thereafter became blind. The readings from his wife made it seem as if his last days were hellish. He died one day before his birthday.

She and I are friends now, or I am honored to believe we are. We volunteered together at our children's school.

God bless you, Anthony! You are missed!

I loved him. I love him still. I love his family.

Not many months later, my own father died of esophageal cancer. He told us on a Thursday. He actually died two Mondays later. I was one of the kids who would go to help care for him for a week. I knew he had cancer for eight days before he died on April 2, 2011. He died the week before I was to come.

All six of us were there. My husband, daughter, and I met one of my sisters at the airport. We rented a car and sped to the hospital. They were going to be turning his life support off at midnight, and we were trying to get there in time. I was speeding because we didn't have much time. And of course, I got pulled over. I felt as if I were lying explaining all this to the officer. I also felt as if I were in some kind of movie. He let us go with a warning. My husband left us at the hospital so he could put our tired four-year-old to bed.

I was in the room when he drew his last breath. I was able to tell, as his heart rate dropped, his pulse slowly dropped, and then the heartbeats became further and further apart. I could barely see the transition from life to death. It would not be long after this that I would fall ill myself. The loneliness, the heartache, the disappointments, and the death had been too much for me to bear.

This was unlike what it was like with my uncle, my mother, and my grandmother during their last moments here on earth.

My uncle had been hit by a crane and died when I was thirteen years old. He had been the father that I didn't have when I was a young girl.

My grandmother's last moments and breaths were definitely violent, as she was suffocating and bubbles were coming out of her mouth while my own mother was yelling at her, pleading with her, really, not to leave her. I was in the room when my mother died too, just ten years prior. I saw it; it was palpable, and there was a somewhat violent twitch as she took her last breath.

Seeing the end of someone's life is an amazing experience. Seeing a fellow human take his or her last breath is sobering, and it is humbling. I was honored to have experienced it each time. I walked out of their room, each time a different person than I when I went in. Someone was physically with me in the world, and then they were not. Each time, I felt more and more thankful that I had another day to live, that it wasn't yet my turn. I even saw the sunlight differently.

I have vowed to make each moment mean something. I want to live each day to the fullest. I am thankful it wasn't over when I thought it might be. I get to hear my daughter's laughter. I get to see her and be with her when she laughs so hard that she can't breathe. I am honored to get more days, and I have gotten more years. I feel as if each day is time that I may not have had, and I want to live it, not waste it. My health has not improved that much. Do I still hurt, physically and emotionally? Yes. And my laughter and my tears are rich with life. I feel it all, and God feels it all through me. I no longer avoid it. I embrace it. I've had heartache, just like everyone

CHAPTER 29

I Do Still Believe

The Lord will fight for you; you need only be still.

—Exodus 14:14 (NIV)

I put myself in a bit of a quarantine when I get run-down to prevent flare ups. I think I do this every four or five months, for a few weeks at a time. I cocoon myself from the rest of the world in an attempt to heal. With the illness, the viruses, the relapses, and the disappointing friendships and relationships, I simply felt I needed to hide from the world, protect what was left, and rebuild. But now when I do it, it is to avoid burnout. It has become a way of life for me. And I get to recharge.

I am in a good place in my home and in my family. My symptoms are improving. I have kept myself from harmful people, places, and things. I am giving myself love daily with good food, good words, self-care, and self-love. So, as my health is slowly improving—at a snail's pace—I am realizing that the healing is an absolute healing. A healing of my emotions, my thoughts, and my physical body. I know that I can live a life in which I am well. Really well! I am not entirely there yet, but I am getting better every single day. It has taken healing all parts of myself though, emotional, mental, and physical. I was not able to skip anything. I could not merely heal my body and ignore the rest. My body was crying for me to help all the parts of myself. My heart wanted so badly to be restored, and I do now see a light at the end of the tunnel.

I'm not sure why it took so long to get quiet, to get still and let God heal me from all of the heartache. I know that as my heart heals, my body will follow. I am excited to see what I can achieve when I am at my fullest potential. I am only sorry that it took such a long and pitiful face dive before I could get still.

In three weeks, two things that I received through visualization have come to me. It was a strange realization when I had it. There they were—I had them. I decided to visualize what I wanted and to test whether this would actually be something that would cause me to manifest things into my own life. I learned that we are all creating our own lives all the time. The job that I thought I had dreamt of and a truck. They were there, in my experience and in my driveway.

I had wanted to work in a church since my college graduation. I had so many things blocking me from that mentally that I never even tried to work in a church or in a ministry of any kind. But I pictured working there every day. I didn't even know in what capacity. It didn't much matter, because picturing and visualizing was simply an experiment at that time. It wasn't long before I received a call that the church administrative assistant was leaving and there was an interim position available. I had been an office manager before and it fit my gifts, so I agreed. I was still sick, so they knew I would only be able to work part-time. I also had my daughter and was not willing to put her in daycare. This fit my needs. And I had always wanted to work in a church environment, and that opportunity presented itself.

Also, I had visualized a truck. I had always wanted to drive a truck, but it seemed silly to want one, so I had only mentioned it years prior as something that might be fun. And I let it go, as nothing I would ever go get for myself, and therefore, I would never likely have one. I was just visualizing it for fun and did not really mention it much more, if at all. I had no resistance to it because it wasn't very important to me at the time. It was just a passing thought.

My husband called me from the GMC dealership one afternoon. I figured he was working, and he said, "Well, I'm buying us a truck, and it's going to be in your name." What? We had not had this conversation. He just went and did this for me. This was so funny to me. I realized that I shouldn't be so surprised. The universe is ready to hand you what you focus attention on, and you never have to tell anyone out there. The opportunities can come to you from anywhere.

Wow! I had seen myself with these things and I have them. I think the only reason it took years to manifest was because I only recently believed that I deserved and was worthy of those things. I have done this many times now. Start small in order to build your confidence. I started doing this with parking places. I was experimenting with this. I felt a little silly, but I kid you not, I almost always get the premium parking spots. It happens so often that when people are riding with me, they will say, "Look, you got the first parking spot." To which I reply, "Yes. I know. I visualized this years ago, and it almost always works out this way for me." You will see that whatever you are putting your thoughts on will come to you, whether you want it to or not. Therefore, try to guard your thoughts.

Yesterday as I was sitting in a hot, humid gym watching and listening to elementary school kids singing with my daughter, I thought, *Wow, am I glad I don't work here.*

See, three years ago, I tried to get a job as a teacher and wasn't hired. I got sick right during that time and wouldn't have been able to teach anyway, but even knowing this, I still was disappointed because they didn't seem to be considering me, and I felt rejected.

Now, though, I am so happy not to be teaching. I am so happy not to be there working. My now fourth-grade daughter would be leaving there after two years for middle school, and that was why I wanted to be there anyway. And being there at six o'clock in the evening would be such a long day, and they weren't done yet.

And when I was working as the church's interim office manager, it was awful. The work was great. The time demands are very difficult and stressful while being ill. But I was surprised to learn that many of the people were not loving. I thought that this too was what I had always wanted only to realize it truly wasn't. So, yes, I got the job I thought I wanted, and it turned out not to fit me at all. And that was great too. Because it was just a step in the journey. And I got to see that just because I think I want something does not mean I actually will once it is in my grasp. I am glad for the opportunity. It was good for me at the time to see that sometimes, what you think you want really isn't. And now that was no longer something I always wanted to do and did not get to do. Gold.

So, here I am—getting it. I finally get it!

It never was better on the other side. The "if I only had this, I would be happy" mentality is *false*. Things were good without pressing for something else. If only it hadn't taken a complete body break down to have this breakthrough. My a-ha moment.

The job, the house, the person—whatever it is, whatever it was—I was never missing out. The pain of having it must have been worse than the pain of not having it, whatever *it* is. And protection is always an answer to prayer. I already had the best of everything within myself. If I don't yet have it manifested, it is on its way.

I hope to be able to live that truth now and for many years to come.

Currently, it is my daughter and myself living this life. We have a wonderful home. Her dad and I co-parent well. We have a wonderful friendship that has overcome the difficulties of divorce. We are friends. And I am truly happy about that.

And friends? I've been through a few. My life took a few turns and with the turns, a few people fell off along the way. The ones that were true friends either never left or made their way back. And now I know who my friends are.

I have since been through a few awesome vehicles and have landed on a Jeep Wrangler, and it feels like it was made for me. I have peace of mind. I am even, dare I say, *happy*. I laugh a lot. I dance. I feel it all—the good and the bad. And I love myself! I do not feel afraid often at all. The trauma may trigger and rear up every now and then. Post-traumatic stress is not an easy condition to navigate, but I am much healthier emotionally and mentally because I have faced it all.

My health? After I began doing the meditation and breath work as energy medicine, my physical health did begin to improve. I still have medical treatments for Lyme disease. But now I understand that everything is working in harmony to heal my mind, body, and emotions. It was never just my body that needed help. I don't know when I will be considered to be in remission, but I know that this, too, is presently being manifested.

I am working again after about four years of not having a consistent job because of my health and life situations. The job I had before this one was temporary. And before that, I was employed with my husband for fifteen years. I was unsure if I could work again and was contemplating disability. But I now work for the doctor who first diagnosed me in 2013. He did not even treat Lyme disease at that time, and now has hundreds of patients at any given time that he actively treats. That was a plot twist and true blessing that I did not see coming. I am truly thankful.

I still don't have all of the answers, but I have a real sense of peace and what I need to do when it feels like the wheels are going to fly off. I go in and spend time in prayer and meditation. I spend time with the inner me, who knows how to get to where I need to be. I no longer look outside myself for a sense of well-being and esteem. It was never there anyway. My inner being knows that I am good enough just the way I am and there is nothing more I need to prove.

I am the answer. I am the hero. And anything that I can't manifest is coming now from the Source who created the Universe. I need only be still.

The End

APPENDIX

A., Van der Kolk Bessel. *The Body Keeps the Score: Brain, Mind, and Body in the Healing of Trauma*. Penguin Books, 2015.

Buhner, Stephen Harrod. *Healing Lyme*. Raven Pr, 2015.

Dooley, Mike. *Top Ten Things Dead People Want to Tell You*. Hay House Inc, 2016.

Dyer, Wayne W. *I Can See Clearly Now*. Hay House Inc, 2015.

Dyer, Wayne W. *The Power of Intention: Learning to Co-Create Your World Your Way*. Hay House, Inc., 2012.

Hicks, Esther, et al. *The Law of Attraction: How to Make It Work for You*. Hay House, 2008.

Hicks, Esther and Jerry: The Teachings of Abraham. *Ask and It Is given: Learning to Manifest Your Desires*. Hay House Publications (India) Pvt. Ltd., 2017.

Makris, Katina I. *Out of the Woods: Healing from Lyme Disease for Body, Mind, and Spirit*. Helios Press, 2015.

Morter, Sue. The Energy Codes: *The 7-Step System to Awaken Your Spirit, Heal Your Body, and Live Your Best Life*. Atria Books, 2019.

William, Anthony. *Medical Medium: Secrets behind Chronic and Mystery Illness and How to Finally Heal*. Hay House Inc, 2017.

Nisargadatta, and Sudhakar S. Dikshit. *I Am That: Talks with Sri Nisargadatta Maharaj*. The Acorn Press, 2012.

Printed in the United States
By Bookmasters